Somebody in Iov u

New Stories from

To Peter & Virginia
— the best inspiration a writer
— or publisher — could have,
all my love

Piers
3.3.93.

PIERS LETCHER

BACKYARD PUBLISHING

First Published in Great Britain in 1993 by Piers Letcher,
Honeypound, Martin, Fordingbridge, Hampshire SP6 3LR.

Distributed in the USA by BackYard Publishing,
RD1 Box 209, Warner, New Hampshire, 03278.

British Library Cataloguing-in-Publication Data.
A catalogue record for this book is available from the British Library.
ISBN 0–9520918–0–1
Somebody in Iowa Loves You

"A Trip Out West", "Saxifrage" and "The Test" were previously published by Raven Arts Press, P.O. Box 1430, Finglas, Dublin, Ireland, and Thistledown Press Ltd., 633 Main St., Saskatoon, SK, S7H 0J8, Canada, in the collection of short stories entitled *The Swimmer In The Deep Blue Dream*, copyright ©1991, Sara Berkeley.

"Static Line Jumping" was previously published by *Words of Wisdom* in December 1992.

Designed by Roderick MacFadyen and Piers Letcher, typeset in Times direct from authors' electronically submitted text. Printed and bound in Great Britain by St. George's Press, Reading, Berkshire.

Contents

The Authors

***Bonnie Randall Schutzman** has been writing since she was in grade school, but only recently figured out that people actually want to read what she writes.*

***Phillip Mannion**, born in 1957 in Manchester, where he lived most of his li(f)e, was educated at universities there, in Italy and in the erstwhile GDR. Entering the computing industry by accident, he spent thirteen years avoiding the cut, but finally succumbed in 1992, five hundred years after Columbus failed to discover India. He has written two collections of short stories and a novel, and passes his days applying for jobs in the Civil Service and eschewing the autobiographical.*

***Charlotte Hebert** has had stories published in* Soundings East *and* Words of Wisdom. *Other stories of hers will soon be published in* Sun Dog: The Southeast Review *and* The Ultimate Writer. *She grew up in Massachusetts, received a BA in psychology from UMASS, Amherst, and currently works part time as a technical writer. With the rest of her time she does what she generally enjoys the most — writing fiction.*

***Ray Davies**, described as "surprisingly sincere", lives in the Lower Haight district of San Francisco, California. He's the unpierced tattooless one. His first story was recently published in the Gollancz anthology 'In Dreams'. His next project will attempt to combine rap music and Language Poetry influences with fantasy genre conventions, or not. People keep telling him he should get a cat.*

***Stan Shursky** realized at an early age that he was born to sleep on the beach in the sun. To this end he dabbled in real estate and software consulting with unsatisfactory results. Recently, he noticed that popular writers like James Michener and Stephen King make a lot of money and live in Maine. He started writing for that reason, though he hopes he will not have to live in Maine.*

***Sara Berkeley** was born in Ireland in 1967. Her two published books of poetry brought her early acclaim and her first collection of short stories, 'The Swimmer in the Deep Blue Dream', was described by*

Karen Beland as possessing "a great sense of expansion and eloquence." Since the summer of 1992 she has been living in California and working, it is thought, on a novel.

***James LaBudde**'s writing helps to rid him, maybe, of strange urges to walk through the subway chattering to the invisible friends playing in his subconscious. Whatever the reason, he has written half a novel, two screenplays and dozens of stories. His stories here hold no hidden meaning, nor do they reflect a particular state of mind or mad moment. They is what they is, whether his invisible friends like them or not.*

***Piers Letcher** was born in 1960, in England, but since 1985 has been based in France. His articles have been published in* Cosmopolitan, The Guardian *and* The Independent, *and his books include 'Europe by Rail', 1985; 'Yugoslavia', 1989; and 'AA Great Train Journeys', 1993. His interests include cycling, skiing and hiking. And good food and fine wine. He travels much more than you'd consider strictly necessary.*

***Lynn Haroutian** lives in Westboro, Massachusetts. She writes prose and poetry to feed the muse, and project plans to pay the rent. Her poetry took first place in the 1991 F. Bals Contest and will be published in 1993 in* The Worcester Review.

***Timothy Martin** is an expatriate American teaching English at Bogazici University in Istanbul. He has been called "a mood writer," which he concurs with wholeheartedly... he only writes when he is in the mood.*

***Melinda Regnell**, born and raised in Maine, writes essays inspired not so much by her degrees and professional experience as by her son. "Children," she says, "See the world so very accurately." She lives in the foothills of the White Mountains of New Hampshire, and has a tendency to live her life to the point of overflowing.*

***Neil Ambrose** was born, raised and lives in the suburbs of north London. He shares a flat with a cat called Daisy and a fish called Cod. On a clear day he can see St. Paul's Cathedral from his kitchen window. He earns his living writing software. 'Tripping Up Snakes' is his first published story. It is dedicated to Winona Ryder.*

Mad Dog

Bonnie Randall Schutzman

She runs in with her braids flying one way and her legs flying the other, catches herself on the corner of the counter just before she slides clear into the refrigerator. Blue-eyed hurricane. Magdalena, little brat. Bitch-in-training.

Mother, Head Bitch, sighs, rolls her eyes to the ceiling. Doesn't scold the kid though. Kid's spoiled rotten. And I'm not just jealous because she gets all the attention.

Kid grabs a cookie. Looks lost without Scamp. Another little brat who couldn't keep his nose out of where he wasn't wanted. Usually porcupines. Last time it was a skunk. Skunk had rabies.

"Hi, Maggie," says Wayne.

Kid stops. Throws her eyes wide like she was in a movie. "Wayne! When did you get here? I thought when you were a monk you had to stay in your cell all the time! I didn't think they'd let you come!"

"Jesuits aren't cloistered, sweetheart." Hugs her hard, kisses her forehead. His cheek's twitching. Not good news.

"Mama said you wouldn't come. She said they wouldn't let you. She said you should stay home where it's quiet."

God. Going to be another one of those weekends.

"Mama can't protect me from myself, sweetheart."

"What's that mean?"

"It means you should say hello to Brent before he thinks you don't love him any more."

Shit. Here she comes. Arms and legs and sunlight braids all flung at me at once, screaming, "Brent! Brent! Oh, Brent, I knew you'd come!" Shoves the cookie in my ear.

"Hey, cut that out. You already deafened me."

Can't stop from hugging the kid. She does that to you. Rather toss her out the window though. Kid laughs and stuffs most of the cookie in her mouth. Around it she says, "What's that in your ear?"

"Chocolate chips, probably."

Laugh like sunshine. "Silly. The sparkly thing. It looks like a diamond."

"That's because it is a diamond."

The Head Bitch rolls her eyes again. "Brent, I've asked you again and again not to wear things like that around the house. It gives Magdalena .entirely the wrong impression of you—"

Wayne grunts. "You mean the right impression."

"In either case, it's not acceptable."

I look at my clothes. Hair combed. Clean t-shirt. Jeans ripped by design, hint rather than display. "Is there something wrong with the way I'm dressed?"

She shudders.

"Don't worry, none of the neighbors are my clients. You don't have to worry I'll be recognized."

"That is not what I meant."

Kid looks from me to her to Wayne, who's got his fingers on the tic in his cheek. His eyes are starting to get that look. Hearing voices again, probably. Gods, demons, angels arguing over his soul. Wonder what makes him think he's so effing important? Angels never argued over my soul. The demons won long ago.

Kid looks back at me, hugs me again. "I think it's pretty. How come I can't get my ears pierced like Brent, huh, Mama? I'm almost eleven, that's old enough for earrings."

I get up. Brat clings to my neck, then lets me drop her. "Want a cookie, Brent? I made them myself. Mama's teaching me to cook. Did she ever teach you to make cookies and stuff?"

"There's not as much need for men to learn how to cook, dear, unless it's something he wants for a hobby."

"But how does he get supper? What do you do for supper,

Brent?"

"I get somebody to buy it for me."

Tinny little silence. I go pour myself another cup of coffee. Lot of things I'd rather have, but they all cost too much and they're starting to get to my brain. I leave them alone now.

Wayne finally clears his throat. Says, "You look like you've been working out."

"Yeah." I leave out the bit about how I pay for it. I leave out the bit about what I take to make the workout work.

Wayne knows, though, because he used to play football before he got religion, before he put that guy in a wheelchair for life, and he gives me a look. It's not the same look as the look he gives me about paying customers.

Head Bitch doesn't know the difference though, so when Bitch-in-training wants to know what gym I go to, Head Bitch says, "That's not something for little pitchers with big ears."

"My ears are not big!" She clamps her hands over them. "They aren't! I don't care what you say!"

"Now, dear. All I said was that you'd look better if you got your hair cut so it fluffed over your ears—"

"That means you think my ears are too big. Do you think my ears stick out, Brent? Do you think they're too big?"

"Like trumpets."

"They do not! You're being mean, all of you. You're—"

Wayne puts his hand on her arm. "He's teasing you." Kid's willing to believe it. "Are you teasing, Brent?"

"She didn't mean that kind of big, anyway. She meant you're nosy about things you aren't supposed to know about, because if you know about them you won't believe the pretty picture she paints of life. She doesn't want you to know that all you get for playing by the rules and doing everything that's expected of you is screwed to the wall."

"Brent! You are not to use language like that in this house."

"Excuse me. What you get for playing by the rules is kicked in the teeth and tossed on the garbage heap."

Wayne closes his eyes, tips his head over the back of the chair. Brat squints at me. "What do you mean, Brent?"

"He doesn't mean anything," says the Head Bitch. "He's just being cynical. He thinks that because his way of coping with his problems is running away and living with the scum of the earth, that means there's something wrong with decent people who try to maintain their standards—"

"Hell of a lot of standards you had when Dad was alive. How many cities were we collecting welfare checks in, three? Or was it four?"

Her cheeks get little pink dots right on the points of her cheekbones, like Snow White's poisoned apple.

Wayne is looking out the window, sort of at the green gauzy curtains and sort of at the silly figurine of a rabbit on a swing that used to be the only toy in the house. Except for the empty beer cans, of course.

The kid twists on her chair. "What does he mean, Mama? We didn't used to be on welfare, did we, Mama?"

"No, dear, we didn't."

"That's a lie." Wayne says it so flat and colorless that at first we don't realize he's spoken.

"Ted and I have never—"

I use a word I don't mean to. I apologize to the kid, who's looking pretty white and scared. "It wasn't you, munchkin. Long before you were born. Why don't you run outside and play now? Isn't Lizzie up by now?"

"She had to go to the beach with her grandmother. Mama, I thought you said only bad people took welfare. Because they were like Brent and wouldn't work."

Wayne, bemused, said, "I wonder what the IRS would do if you put down 'hustler' as a profession."

"They haven't audited me yet."

Could almost believe there was a flash of sympathy.

Our mother goes to Magdalena and puts her arms around her. "Life was very hard before you were born, sweetheart. Brent's father wasn't a good man, and—"

"He sure the fuck was better than you! At least he never pretended he was holy and pure. What about that fat bloke with the spots on his hands, the one who used to spank us for making too much noise while you were up in the bedroom? The one who bought us the car, and the sofa? What's the difference between that and what I do? Is merchandise more moral than cash?"

"There's nothing wrong with accepting gifts from a lover."

"You hated his guts."

Her eyes fill with tears. "You were only four. You can't remember. You don't know what you're taking about."

"Can't forget, is more like it."

Wayne stands up. "Don't judge her, Brent. Only God has the right to judge."

"It sure as hell doesn't stop her from judging me. And trying to blame it all on a man whose only fault was trying too hard — what did she ever do to help? Always nag, nag, nag, how are we going to pay for Brent's doctor, Cissie needs a new coat, I'm so ashamed to have my mother see that old beat-up refrigerator and that old beat-up car."

"What's wrong with wanting a nice life for my children? Just because you don't appreciate it."

Wayne puts his hands on my shoulders. "Sit down, kid."

"Don't think you can boss me around just because you're bigger than me." I sit down anyway, with coffee.

He hands me a cookie, grins. "No. Because I'm older than you and meaner than you. What's Cissie going to think if we get in a fight on her big day?"

"Don't you like my cookies, Brent?" says the brat.

"Not for breakfast."

Mother is starting to put the dishes in the dishwasher. Her hands are shaking.

"So there's nothing wrong with accepting gifts from a lover. There's nothing wrong with taking a lover you hate. What am I doing wrong? Is it the cash, or don't I keep them long enough?"

"We can't talk about it in front of the child. She's too young."

I look at Wayne. I look at the brat. I look at my mother.

I remember hiding under the stairs while she screamed at my father, while she hit him with the broom or the pot or whatever she had in her hand, until he had to hit her back. I remember crawling upstairs after her, knowing if he saw me he'd blame me too, and asking her if she was alright, and her saying in a distant tired voice, "You're too young to know about things like that."

Wayne's looking out the window again, not paying any attention. He never did pay any attention. Like those voices in his head are more real than any people out here.

I remember thinking, it must be something I did. It must be because I'm stupid. Then later, when I knew what was wrong with me — he must have seen it before I did.

"All right, I know I'm no good. Okay?"

"Then why don't you change? Come home, go back to school, get your degree like Cissie's doing. I'm sure Ted would pay for it. We'd be so proud to see you up there the way we saw Wayne, the way we're going to see Cissie tomorrow, and Maggie—"

"Not me," says the brat. "I'm going to join Mother Teresa and help take care of the poor."

"She'll be dead by then," I say. Wayne looks at her, then goes back to looking at the curtain.

"Don't be absurd," Mother tells her. "You'll go to college and you'll pursue a respectable career."

The brat tells her, "I'd rather go to heaven."

Wayne's shoulders shake, like he wants to laugh. Mother scowls. She turns to me. "Will you, Brent? Please? It would mean so much to us. We'll even leave you alone about — that. We won't talk about girls for you."

"That?" says Magdalena, pausing with a cookie in midair.

"She means about my being gay," I answer, before I realize she probably doesn't want me to be so blunt in front of the kid. I'm right, she nearly has a hernia on the spot. Too shocked to even squawk.

Wayne asks the kid, "Do you know what that means?"

She dips her cookie in her milk and takes a bite. "That he's going to die soon?"

"What? What do you mean?" I've had religious wackos tell me God is going to zap me, but Maggie's a little young for that and it's not her style anyway.

"AIDS," she explained.

"Oh. No. I'm not planning to, anyway. I'm careful." Wayne asks,

"Always clean needles? Even in the gym?"

I nod. Wayne looks dubious. Mother looks like she's going to kill us both. At last she tells him, "You're as bad as Brent for not thinking before you expose the child to the evil side of life."

"Don't you think that if you had told us the truth about why Dad was always sick, and told us the truth about how he died, and told us the truth about where the money was going, and done something besides try to make excuses for him, we might all have grown up a little happier?"

Mother doesn't think so and she says so, very waspishly. "You have to protect the little ones. One careless word and you can damage them clear to the soul."

"And you'd rather have us think you're a liar and a cheat?"

She goes white. "You don't think that too?"

"I try not to judge you. But I know you lied to us. For our own good, for the best of motives, but still a lie. Look what you've done to Brent. You succeeded in protecting Father. You succeeded so well that Brent won't believe the truth even now. You wanted him to think ill of you rather than his father, and he does. But what damage does it do to a child's soul to think his mother lied and cheated and stole? To know that she lied and cheated and stole to protect a man who beat her and beat them?"

"She provoked him!"

He gestures at me, and I sit down. Mother's got her hands to her eyes, her back to us. The kid looks at me. "She doesn't lie to me."

I shrug. Wayne says, "Sure. Did she tell you what happened to Scamp?" "He got hit by a car," the kid replies, puzzled. "She forgot to latch the gate and he got out and — why are you looking at me like that?"

I put my hand on hers. "Do you know what rabies is, kid?"

She frowns. "It makes wolves go crazy. I read about it in a book."

"And a wolf is a cousin of a dog, right?"

She nods.

"It's a very painful disease, kid. It makes the dog sick, and it makes him so he can't see or think, and he can't recognize the people he loves. All he knows is how it hurts, and he lashes out to try to make the pain better. He doesn't even know who he's hurting."

"And Scamp had that?"

"Remember the skunk that sprayed him?"

She wrinkles her nose. "Remember? Phew! I had to scrub him!"

"Skunks sometimes carry rabies. This skunk bit Scamp. I think that's why he killed the skunk. I helped Mom take them both to the vet, and the vet put Scamp in a cage and took good care of him while they tested the skunk, and when we knew the skunk was sick, we had the vet put Scamp to sleep so he wouldn't get sick and be in pain and hurt himself and us."

About halfway through, tears start rolling down her face, but she's calm enough. "That's all?"

I nod.

Wayne hands her his handkerchief. She blows her nose.

"Why didn't you tell me, Mom?"

"I didn't want you to be upset. I wanted to make it easier for you."

Magdalena's not the kind to throw a tantrum. She just sort of walks out. But she stops at the door. "Thanks, Brent." Screen door slams behind her. We hear her sobbing on the porch. Mother walks out the other door, back to wherever it is she spends her days. Wayne looks at me. I look at him.

"You could be talking about yourself."

I shrug. "Gonna take me to the vet to put me out of my misery?"

"I don't think you've got anything incurable."

"God, don't start on me with that religious kick."

"I wasn't going to. I wasn't going to tell you to move back home and I certainly wasn't going to tell you to stop living with that dancer."

He stops. Makes me ask, "May as well tell me and get it over with."

"How about doing something to make yourself happy instead of what makes Mom the maddest?"

"She sits there condemning everything I do, everything I think, what I am. Blames me for believing her, blames me for everything. What the fuck am I supposed to do, give in?"

"No, you don't understand. Do what you want. Don't think about her at all. Not whether she approves, not whether she understands, not whether she caused it. Or whether any of us approve."

"Easy for you to say."

"You think she liked it when I quit the Bengals and went into the priesthood? Went from 'my son the NFL star' to 'my son who's living next door to a crack house in San Francisco?'"

Can't say I ever thought about it. I shrug.

His cheek's jumping again and he's trying to stop it. He looks more like he wants to get up and jump around with it. I start to pretend I don't notice. And then that's lying about it too. So I ask, "You okay? You look like you should be in the hospital."

"I'll manage. I'm on a new medication and it seems to be helping so far. But it's heavy-duty stuff and I space out."

"Coffee?"

"Thanks." Then, "You never asked me that before." I know he doesn't mean the coffee.

I shrug and go get a cookie.

Big Blue Sky

Bonnie Randall Schutzman

John stops his pickup in the driveway. A plume of dust settles around him.

There is no gate, just a cattle guard with a few weeds growing up through the bars. The sign overhead proclaims 'Wallace Angus' but the cattle dotting the field are red and square, like bricks. Some newfangled Swiss breed. John doesn't look at them when he gets out of the truck. He doesn't look at the mountains, white already in September.

September the dry, September the dead, when nothing is real but dust and wind and the nights of frost. Frost to the soul, by God. Ice in the bones.

His mother named him Yanni, but he became John when he got to school. His grandmother said their name wasn't Wallace, either, but Walechec or something like it that the immigration agents couldn't understand. Now that he would like to know, his mother doesn't remember.

The last rain was a thunderstorm in August. Dust covers the rocks beside the road and coats the chokecherry bushes growing in the barrow pit behind the barn. With the leaves gone you can read the ad painted on the back: Morton's Shoeblack, shine like a mirror, and a skinny black boy looking at his surprised reflection in the toe.

John opens the mailbox, which hangs at an odd angle atop a twisted post made from a branch of juniper, gray, weathered. He thumbs through the circulars. Nothing special today. He folds them over, shoves them in the hip pocket of his greasy jeans, tosses his cigarette into the road. A thread of smoke marks where the butt still burns.

He spins gravel from the tires when he shoves the truck into gear. The bag of groceries on the seat beside him jingles with cans against glass. The toolbox clatters in back as he jounces over the ruts. Dust, brown grass, rusted barbed wire broken here and there on the juniper posts. The house is right below him, but the road follows the ridge for a mile before it drops into the valley.

Gophers poke up from their mounds like little pegs. Magpies flash black and white, seeking maggots in the rotting cowpies. Cattle with manure on their sides stand around the water trough, hunt for shade under the windmill. Circle Q cattle, not his.

He stops the truck at the fence, gets out to open the gate, drives through, gets out to shut the gate. The gate is only a post held by two loops of barbed wire. A barb cuts his finger. He sucks it briefly, but it tastes of transmission oil — burned transmission oil from a car run too long under too much load by a California tourist with more money than brains. Too bad the garage got all the pretty pennies the tourist paid to get it fixed.

John hates the garage, but it pays. Cattle don't.

He likes the way the Yellowstone river sparkles between bands of gray boulders, blue water reflecting the big blue sky. He does not look at the jagged teeth of the mountains behind.

A 707 crashed up there years ago, trying to land in Bozeman in a storm. They knew where it went down, knew within a mile or less. But the blizzard hid the wreckage, and spring branches hid the broken ones, and wind and ice and rain erased the scars on the rocks. Some rock-climbers stumbled across it years later.

Where the road loops down to the valley, a few posts stick up through the sagebrush and greasewood. Gravestones, fenced in by pickets so the cattle won't rub them over, lilacs that bloom in the spring beside a stone-filled pit. Somebody's farm, prosperous and happy. Graves for two women, seven children, one man.

He wonders how long the last survivor waited after the wars and the funerals before he packed up and left. How long before he got tired of empty walls and wondering why after fighting, fighting,

fighting for bread, for a roof, for a paycheck, giving up the horses and then the cattle and finally even the fields, and all so the kids could have schooling, why after all that she blamed him for it, as if a man could help it if sometimes it got to him and he filled the hollow with beer so the wind wouldn't echo past his heart, if he sometimes lashed out.

Would have lashed out at someone else if there was someone else there.

John shoves the black baseball cap with the Caterpillar logo back on his head. Not much hair there now. Not much hope of finding a woman to help a little when the wind got bad.

Tom won't forgive him either. "You drove Ted away," Tom says. "You killed him."

As if bullets in Panama were John's fault. Chance a man took when he went into the army. Nobody's fault, nobody's at all, 'cept maybe the generals who got us into it, hacks and crooks scoring each other off in front of the TV cameras. Nothing a man can do about that. They say go, you go. Ted went.

Tom at least calls sometimes, from that restaurant of his up on the High Line. Doing well, from the sound of it. Elise doesn't call. John isn't sure where she is or what she's doing, and Tom won't tell. "Not after what happened," he says.

What's a man to do when his own children and his woman all turned against him?

John parks the truck in the yard beside the station wagon. The wagon is up on blocks, and weeds grow up around the rusty brakedrums. He sold the tires and the wheels last winter. No use letting them go to waste.

He gets out. He drags the sack across the seat. The brown paper crumples in his fingers. It tears. He tosses the shred aside and rolls the top down a bit. Cheap bags, won't even hold a six of beer and couple of cans of beef stew any more.

Can't count on anything any more.

The Famous Ninth of May!

Phillip Mannion

One thousand, eight hundred and twenty six days. It can seem a lifetime. On the eve of your fifth birthday, it is a lifetime.

"I'll be five tomorrow. I wonder what time it is? It might be tomorrow already, I wish I could tell what time it is, it must be *thirty* o'clock by now. I wonder what I'll get? It might be a football, I'd like a football. My dad will play with me then when he gets home."

The alarm was due to go off at half-past five, but he is awake again before it rings. He is always awake before it rings.

"Better turn this thing off, don't want it to wake her up. Or the kids. Anyway, an extra five minutes now makes no odds. Oh, my! Stiff as a board — we need a new bed, I reckon, but there's no chance of that."

Three young children, a wife and a mother-in-law to feed on one miner's wages, and how far can you stretch a pound-a-week rise?

"Never mind, soon be holidays. I'll go off hay-making on Chat Moss, that'll be enough for something new, and at least I'll be outside. Better get up I suppose. 'Tea for breakfast today, Sir?' 'Yes, please.' 'And eggs and bacon?' 'Oh, yes, and fried bread!' 'And will you cook it, Sir?' 'Not on your nelly!' Oh well, cornflakes again then."

"Who's that moving about? Must be my dad, he must be going to work. That means it's morning! That means it's today, my birthday! Happy birthday to me, squashed tomatoes for tea, bread and butter in the gutter, happy birthday to me! I suppose I'd better stay in bed though, he wouldn't like it if I got up so early."

"Another day... another dollar, at least that's what they say. But it's never a shiny, silver dollar — not down the pit, it's not. I wonder how my birds are doing? Morning, birds! I won't lift the cover though, they'll start nattering and wake everybody up. Just a little peek under here, then! Hello Darkie, hello Sam! Well, it's arrived at last, young un's birthday. Perhaps he'll shut up now! Dad, Dad, can I have this? Can I have that? Dad, can I have a football? Well, he'll get a football later on. I suppose that means I'll have to have a game with him when I get home. Anyway, time for the off. Morning everybody! Happy birthday, Phillip!"

"BANG! Front door shutting. He always says he tries to shut it quiet, but he never manages. Morning Dad! Happy birthday, Phillip! Go back to sleep now."

"Two miles to walk at six in the morning. It'd drive you daft if you thought about it. I wonder if I could sleep as I walk along? Better not try, I might manage it, fall over and hurt myself. Where would we all be then, eh? So — what'll I think about as I walk along, to try and stay awake? Well, Leigh play Wigan tonight, last match of the season. I'd like to go and see it, but I'll probably not get the chance on Phillip's birthday... I could *think* about being asleep! Now, now behave! Anyway, it's downhill now, down Parr Brow, happen I'll run? Happen I'll run up the other side as well, when I get over Ellenbrook? That's the problem with valleys, I reckon, what they call a *design fault*. Eh, that's deep for this time of the morning! The Pitman Philosopher on his way to work!

"Here comes the first train taking coal over to Wigan. I bet they're warm on that footplate. Not that it's cold for me, these May mornings. Done your eighty-hour fortnight, lads? Nearly? Good for you! Have a pint for me at lunch-time! Speaking of which... The Royal Oak. It's gone quick today, Peter lad. I'll stop in and have a pint myself on the way back.

"Did you know, Peter, did you know...? Well, yes, actually, I did know. In fact it was me that told me! Eh, but what a good idea, eh? That extra half-hour opening in the afternoons so that the pitmen can have a pint on their way home. Brilliant — local magistrates and pitmen at one! Makes a change.

"But not today, I'm afraid... Phillip's football.

"And there it is! Mosley Common Pit! Pride of the Lancashire coalfield, the most modern pit, though not the biggest. The best for me, though, and I've been down a few. Years of coal down there, and it's dry. Not like Astley Green, that was a cold, wet hole — up to your chin in it most of the time. There's nothing worse than wet... except bad roof. Now, that would drive you daft!"

Gibfield, Astley Green, Mosley Common. He was a Bevan Boy, one of Lady Astor's Earthworms, missed the War because he was scrabbling underground in a two-foot seam, listening to the roof — listening to the roof.

"Chris! Chris! Wake up! Is it time to get up yet? Oh, I'm sorry. Perhaps if I think hard enough I'll wake my mam up. Wake up, mam! Wake up! Can't hear her. Who's that snoring? It must be my Nanny. Perhaps I'll say I'm not so well, so I won't have to go to school today. Perhaps my mam'll play football with me, she's good at football. I could have a pie at dinner-time, it'd be better than school dinners! WAKE UP EVERYBODY!"

"And down it goes! WHOOSH! Hang on to your guts, lads, you're on your way to Hell! If only you knew it. But you do know it — if only *they* knew it up there. What's black and sore and sweaty all over? A pitman on his way back up from work. Damn, I've forgot my snap! Have I? Better check. No, there it is. Corned beef sandwiches and an apple. It tastes like caviare when you eat it down here — it *looks* like caviare when you eat it down here!"

"Breakfast time at last! Can I go outside, please Mam, and play with my football? But I'm not hungry this morning! Well, can I stay at home today and play football, and can Peter stay as well? Oh, well. I wonder if they'll know at school if it's my birthday? I wonder if the headmaster will tell everybody at assembly and then they'll all sing Happy Birthday? OK then, I'll go."

"Break at last. Eeeeh, stretch, eh? This is a funny one. I'll be glad to see the back of it; it's so low I end up having to crouch down to get at the roof and rip it down. It makes you ache, too, I can tell you, twisting round and squatting down and picking, picking, picking at the roof. Not half-way through yet either, I'll be glad to see the back of it.

"Just have one butty. Now where did I leave my bag? Aye, there it is. Better not be any mice in there today, not after the morning I've had. Well, if you've got a mouse in your kitchen, Missus, never mind about getting a cat — just send for a pitman and tell him it's the brother of the one ate his snap this morning — he'll catch it for you! The world's best mouser — a pitman with his snap gone! I wonder who told 'em about sandwiches? I wish they'd eat coal dust instead, like we do.

"Anyway, none in there today. Cup of tea? Yes, Peter, I will. Thank you very much. Who're you working with today? On your own again, are you? Well, watch out then in them low seams! I'd like a change if I could get one. I wish someone would let 'em know I'm looking.

"See that one? Look at it! Big as a rat! What do they live on, can't be just jam butties."

As lunch-time approaches, there is an air of expectation in the minds of all who work. In offices people are looking forward to the daily trip to the pub, a chance to forget the tedium of the morning. Factory workers, more tired by physical effort or more mentally numbed by the dreadful monotony of their divided labours, look forward to sitting for half-an-hour or three quarters in their canteen — the management separate from those they manage. For the five-year-old boy, there is the excitement of pretending his school-dinner is a party. For the miner, there is only heat, dust and fatigue. The miner is tired, but the coal is implacable in its adversity. It doesn't stop for lunch.

"I wonder what he's doing now? Sums, or reading? Or history? That's the one, know how we got here, so that we can go somewhere else. Could be music, he's always singing that song — 'The whistling gypsy came over the hill, down to the valley shady, he whistled and he...' Anyway, soon be over. Just *DIG*, this pick *IN*, a *FEW* more *TIMES*, aaand *PULL* the coal *DOWN*, in these *STINK*ing old *MIIINES*."

He sighs.

"Any second now the bell's going to go."

"Any second now the hooter'll go."

Any second now the roof's going to go.

"My old man's a pitman, he wears a pitman's hat..."

"I sup*POSE* for your *PRES'NT* I'd give you the *SUN*, so you're not down *HERE* where you *WATCH* the mice *RUN*... What's that? A crack? The roof? (***WATCH*** the mice ***RUN***!) Run. ***RUN! R U U N!***"

How far can a man run in less than a second? How strong are his ribs? How thick is his blood? The black fist of the mine crushes him like a screaming black and red fly. No time for the bladder to empty, no time for goodbyes, no time for his world to flash before his dust-rimmed eyes. In seconds they ring the bell that makes the miners shiver, that makes them glad it's not them, that makes them go where only fools would go. They do not wait for the Rescue Team, they do not wait for death. The great, black tombstone is lifted by six men, and the half-living man tenderly, tenderly moved clear. GET HIM OUT! UP THE SHAFT! WIPE HIS FACE! GET HIM SAFE!

Who'll tell his wife?

"I'd give you the sun, I'd give you a breeze, but what is all this stuff, why can't I breathe? Salt in my mouth, wet warm salt. Dreaming, wake up, why can't I breathe?"

"Why, Uncle? Why am I going to your house? It's my birthday — shouldn't I go home? How long will I stay? And where's my mam? And my football? and where's my Dad?"

"I'd give you the sun... I'd give you... But now there's nothing left to give. And what would you give me?"

"Breath, and sunny days, and time to play."

Extreme unction, oil to prepare the soul for a journey. A woman too shocked for shock, children too little to shock. Too little to leave. Not dreaming, not waking, not breathing, just dying — Why can't he breathe? Wouldn't you breathe? Didn't he breathe?

A Priest's Tale

Phillip Mannion

As the young priest flung open the door to the sacristy he started to wish us a cheery "Good morning!" but had got only as far as the "Goo" when he fell off the step down into the little, cramped room. "Shit!" he spat out as he landed on the floor. It was the first complete word I'd heard the man say, and it wasn't exactly what I'd come to expect from men of the cloth.

My vision of priests had been based on the old fellows who had been our parish priests over the last few years. They had all been harmless old sorts who didn't do too much, but seemed idyllically content with their queer little jobs.

For that's what it was of course. Not a nine-to-fiver, not nearly so strenuous. They did have to get up in time for early mass at eight every day, but they lived next door to the church and couldn't eat before the mass, so they could lie in their pits till five before. It's true they had three masses on Sundays, and didn't finish work till after the benediction at eight in the evening. But this was in the days of the Tridentine mass, and they just mumbled away to themselves with their backs to the congregation. Everybody knew that when he did a bit of a hand-jive and said, "Hic hoc hoolie holie holie," they all had to genuflect, and then when he genuflected they had to say, "Ipsit dixit quixit fixit." But whether there were the same number of hic hocs at eight at night as there were at eleven in the morning was a matter for conjecture, and what did it all mean anyway?

Sometimes at the early mass the altar boy would be the only one there to listen for any fluffed spells, but we weren't the boys to point them out. See, if you served mass, you could eat the sandwiches you'd brought with you for breakfast afterwards and be late in to school. So, "Excuse me, Father, but shouldn't there have been three sha na nas there? And just what is the ablative ending again?" — all that was right out.

And when they weren't on stage, what did they do? Many a night I would wander past the presbytery and look up at the lights shining through the curtains. I could imagine the scene inside:

The house-keeper has just finished clearing away after he'd wolfed the meal she'd cooked. The old fellow's on his second cup of tea, listening to the news on the wireless. Later on he'll wander down to the kitchen to make some cocoa to knock back while he does *The Telegraph* crossword and listens to the late news on the wireless. But what use would they put all this worldly knowledge to? "Take three Hail Marys a day, and the pain will go and the Bomb will be de-invented."

But that's the cynic of today smirking. At the time I thought the life sounded wonderful, and the priests were a race apart from the grimy-lashed pitmen, and the women deafened in cotton mill carding-rooms who made up the rest of my hometown's population. I decided that if the choice was the coal-face or the altar to kneel before there was little to think about.

One day a priest came round to our school and did a spiel on being a missionary in Africa or somewhere. "Any boy who wants to be a priest please come out of the classroom now, and we'll talk about it." I was there like a shot, first in the queue. Did I want to be a priest? Of course I did, all those funny kaftan things in green and gold? Right up my street. And then he asks me, "And is this the first time you've considered the priesthood, my son." "Yes, Father, it is," I replied. "Then you just go away and think about it for a while, and next time we're here we'll talk again. If you're still interested in a year or two, we'll see."

So that was it. All the other smart alecs in the queue behind me said, "Oh no, Father, I've been thinking about this for years." Had they buggery — they'd just got sharp ears and quick wits was all. And then they all got the weekend away at the seminary, while I got

As True As I'm Riding This Bicycle

Phillip Mannion

There's a lot of crap talked, really. At least I think it's crap. You know, you've all met 'em. People who know someone who was in the crowd when Kennedy got shot; people who have had strange memories from other lives — I've never met anyone who actually thinks he was Oswald, but I've had a few pints with nutters who think they were Kennedy. Or the clever bastards you get noshing up Brick Lane these days. "You do agree with the deconstructivist theories of multicultural town planning, don't you? Or are you a complete wanker?" Intellectual they call themselves. Interfucking-mission, more like — a loada people out taking the piss.

The one that gets me the most is when some geezer in a boozer says his friends call him Big John. "And," he adds with a wink, "my girl-friends know why." You know, he's like six feet three and twenty stone. Any fucker knows why. Then he says, "Ever had sex with more than one woman at once?"

Now this really pisses me off. I mean, even having sex with one woman twice in one night would be an achievement, and he says, "I had six once." Come, did you? I asks, but he's off onto the details, which frankly leave me cold. Whatever it is people say, it's a load of crap. With one exception.

Me. I saw a ghost once. Now, I know that that's a bit out, like the kids these day are more into leaving ghostly bloody images behind them as they hammer some twat's Cosworth faster than the speed of light down the High Street, but I have actually seen a ghost.

It was like this.

Me 'n' Tracey had been out for a curry after we'd had a few with the lads. The Hammers had stuffed the Yids three-nil, so talk about Bubbles, or what? Well, it was her birthday and I wanted to do something special for her, so when the pubs shut we went to the local Paki for a plate or two of slap-up. And a few more drinks to wash it down with.

Well, after that we wended our way home, as they say, with a few more Bubbles to keep the spirits up, and it was straight upstairs for a friar. What? Friar Tuck. Anyway, I says to her, "Get your gear on, doll," and she says, "Fuck off — it's me bleedin' birthday. I'm not getting slagged up for any cunt. It's bloody cold, anyway." And she puts her best woolly nightie on. Well, I ask you. Would you? No, and me neither, so I puts me head on the Armadillo, and it's Zedsville, Comatosa here I come.

Well, a pint's a pint, no matter what, and I don't know how many I'd had, but I'd been thinking we'd celebrate her birthday with a bit of how's your father, so Nelson bleeding Riddle, known to his friends as Jimmy, didn't enter into it. And I fell asleep.

Later on, God knows what time it was, I woke up with this throbbing bladder and a voice inside me head like a tap running. I gets out of bed and starts making me way, doubled up, to the bog. Just as I get to the foot of the bed there's this ghost coming towards me, all white and wavy and weird. "No!" I screamed, and jumped backwards onto the bed, lying there doubled up with me legs in the air and my hands over me face.

"Trace!" I shouted, "It's a ghost!"

"Don't be so bleeding stupid," said the ghost, "and get off my side of the bed, will you?" It seems that my beloved had also been called to the bathroom, and was on her way back when I mistook her for a spectral visitor. I lay there for a while, whimpering, then I rocked myself off the bed and crawled off for a slash, agony dogging my every kneestep. I get to the bleeding loo, and by now I can't stand up at all. I try holding the old fellow high enough, but the best I could do was stick it through the gap below the loo seat, and that was at a pinch, if you know what I mean. So I reach up and grab the cistern to pull myself up. There's this loud creaking, groaning sound as the bloody thing comes away from the wall.

"What's that creaking?" I hear Tracey shout.

"It's the bloody ghost again," I call back, "moaning." But at least I'm collapsed on the bog now and weeing to my heart's content. "Aaah," I sigh with relief.

"What's..."

"The ghost, the ghost, Trace," I tell her. I'll worry about the truth in the morning, like most men.

Well, that's my story and I'm sticking to it. Bit of a slash in the pan, perhaps, but more likely than having sex with six women at once. Unless you actually really had been Kennedy, that is.

The Obligatory Oriental Story

Phillip Mannion

I had reached that point in my career as writer, thinker, man, at which I felt it necessary to write an Oriental story. They had all done it, of course. They, you know — Hesse, Barthelme, Grey. And now me.

Being an obsessive and perfectionist, I knew I would first need to assimilate the East, in all its forms, generations and locales. A crank might have actually wanted to become a chink, but I would have condescendingly pointed out to such a simulated slit-eye, a pale ghost with a pig-tail, that this is bloody fiction, not life.

An army marches on its stomach, and a writer writes on his bottom, so I booked a table at my local Chinese and ordered a Set Meal For One. Soon I was an expert in Chinese nosh, whatever the region — from the Western Deserts to the South China Seas — and whatever the numbering system: "Yo! Chinee Johnee! You bring me one 27, one 10110 and a double FFF." Gourmet, gourmand and numerologist in one tasteful, throw-away package.

But man shall not write on a crispy duck alone, and while I waited for the Dim Sum trolley to pass I read philosophy, history, poetry. I knew Confucius better than his mother, and I found peace beneath a big old tree.

This phase took some time, it took some time I will admit, for the dead weight of Indo-European tongues made my fingers cack-handed with the brush, even though I knew the word for 'literature' in three dozen Sino-Tibetan languages. But when my fingers were gnarled as the willow tree, and I knew in my aching joints that I had the soul of a yellow man inside me, with shaking strokes I wrote:

'One bright day in summer the prince sat in the cool shade of a great, green tree. He took from the simple canvas bag he had packed himself a three-string fiddle, and began to pluck a soothing tune. A wasp landed on his hand, and stung him sharply there. The prince stroked the wasp's head tenderly, smiled and said — Fly on, little tiger of the air, fly on.'

And when my story was done I laid down my brush, slipped the manuscript into a sepia envelope and sent it to Wilson, Chauncey and Chang, specialist publishers of oriental interest books.

The moon had not yet changed his mantle but half a dozen times when back came the reply, "We regret we cannot use your story at this time."

I was jolted out of my complacence. I had felt sure I had the essence of the Orient in sixty-seven words, but I had failed. No reason was given in their ten words which captured the essence of the Occident as I had experienced it, but when I reflected on my vision of the East I found only great mounds of steaming rice and irrelevant old catch-phrases. Confucius he say. But Wilson, Chauncey and Chang were smart cookies, fortune cookies, and they knew that old China was no longer the heart of the Orient. I must look further East, into the red eye of the sun, I must look to Japan.

I then set about assimilating Japan, ancient and modern. An exemplary diet of raw fish and rice wine was enjoyed while I watched every episode of Shogun on video. Kurosawa was next, and was like rice wine to the raw scaly stuff of the television melodrama. Shogun did help me with my Japanese though — Kanichi-wa, wakari-mas, ee-ay, and Japanese word par excellence and ideal for the acting abilities of the cast of Shogun, the word for yes — hai, pronounced gutturally and short — hai.

But this was in one third of my leisure time — the other thirds were taking a long bath the wrong way round (wash first, rinse off the soap then get in the tub) and, most excellent fun of all, karaoke. I could belt out a version of 'My Way' that would melt the snows of old Mount Fuji. Twenty minutes each per day, rotated to avoid staleness; that was leisure. The real day was work. I had two jobs, one in finance and one in electronics. I could quote the opening and closing prices of the Nikkei (and the Hang Seng, just for fun) every day for the whole of the previous three years, at the same time as building very small televisions and enormous computers. Twelve hours dosh and eleven hours tosh, that was me — you can't do the tosh without the dosh, so I gave that a little more time, but both got maximum effort.

Was I ready? No, I still had cetacean to eat, the tea ceremony to attend, geishas to be serenaded by, and martial arts to master. Some of this I did in slow motion, to avoid the danger of injury, some at break-neck speed. Eating the whale, for example. (I refused to eat dolphin, considering it immoral to eat something more intelligent than me.)

At last I was ready. I bought a word processor, mastered the Kanji keyboard, and delicately depressed the little grey pads:

'I wrestle Sumo,
Then yens I make in millions
Drenched in perfumo.'

I called it 'Haiku for New Nippon', and sent it off to Wilson, Chauncey and Chang. Within the transmission time of a trans-global electronic share deal, the reply came back by electronic mail: "We regret that we are unable to use your piece at the moment."

I sat immobile for what seemed like several incarnations, head in hand, considering my mistakes. I had had thesis and antithesis, but where could I find the synthesis? Not ancient China, not modern Japan. What then? The answer came with a great cry, like the whisper of a thousand million voices: China now!

And so I immersed myself in Marx and Mao. Strict discipline entered my life, none of this one hour a day for leisure, none of this bourgeois bathing in warm water. Thought and action became worthy of a communist cadre, and I worked ceaselessly for the revolution. I had good contacts in The Forbidden City, but my constant studying enabled me also to be accepted by the students of Tien-an-Mien Square. They could have used me as a go-between, but my inscrutability was too complete, and no-one knew I held the fate of the country in my hands.

Instead they rolled the two-sided die — 'Now the Great Leap

Forward!' or 'Now the Great Fall Back!' "Snake eyes!" I cried, but they couldn't hear me above the roar of the tanks. "Do not pass Go," I cried again, but the shrieks of the students drowned my words, soaked my manuscript in their blood and their tears. "Do not collect two hundred dollars," I whispered in the dawn that followed, "do not send anything to Wilson, Chauncey and Chang."

The voice of modern China shall be my story now; a quiet voice, a stilled voice.

October, 1990

Static Line Jumping

Charlotte Hebert

They've been talking about going sky diving out of Pepperell again at work. Or not sky diving exactly — where you jump out of a plane, and you free-fall for close to a minute, and after all that, you pull open your own 'chute — but more like static line jumping. That's what it's officially called when you're a beginner. With static line, your 'chute is opened for you so you don't have to think about it.

Which makes the utmost sense to me.

They've been talking about it a lot — in the morning when we go for coffee and danish downstairs in the cafeteria, at lunch in sub shops and burger joints, on breaks as we smoke butts out on our company's wooden deck. Only two of them have gone so far — Gerry and Matt — but they're trying to convince the rest of us. Gerry has gone three times so far, and Matt, he's coming up to his sixth. Once he makes six he'll graduate to a kind of beginner free-fall — but I'm not even ready to imagine that. With free-fall, of course, unlike with static line, you pull open your own 'chute. With beginner free-fall you start from ten-to-twelve thousand feet up, and you fall for seven seconds, and you count: one-one-thousand, two-one-thousand, three-one-thousand. On four-one-thousand you look for the ripcord, on five-one-thousand you reach, on six you pull, and on seven you're sailing pretty.

So they say.

Matt has this thing about trying to flip people out when he talks about it all. He describes the static line experience really meticulously, down to the last singular detail. He goes through an entire routine, and the whole time he just kind of stands back, even as he's telling it, and laughs. He doesn't laugh out loud — it's more like it's going on somewhere inside. Like it's going on in his eyes as he exchanges knowing looks with Gerry, and it's going on as he flips back his head. You couldn't be mad at him about it though — not Matt. Not him. He's more of just this mirthful guy, more just trying to enjoy himself a little, to spook somebody. But if you ever need to sit out with him on his back porch 'till 3am, if you ever need to get counsel on something or maybe just fly off with him on his motorcycle in the middle of the work-a-day world — he's there.

Anyway, this whole thing lately, it's been just zinging around in my mind. The other day we went to Stan's sub shop for lunch. This new guy, Kamran, just started working with us — a golden opportunity if ever there was — so Matt started in.

We were squooshed into one booth, the six of us, and the paper wrappings our subs came in overlapped so that I ended up eating Lucy's onions. Matt leaned forward across the Formica table toward Kamran. "Kamran," he said, "imagine this," — and to begin his palms were held vertically up in the air. "You're in a plane. It's about four by eight in diameter, and you're crammed inside with four other guys. On your back is your 'chute," he said, pointing to Kamran's back, "and you're strapped in so tight, and you're so conscious of this thing's bulky humongous mass, that it feels like you're wearing a dead weight.

"There's just one small thing connecting you and that 'chute to safety. Just one thing preventing you from falling to your death with a splat like the most insignificant bug against my Harley." And here, Matt clapped his hands together piercingly to make the splatting sound, then paused long and hard for effect. "Just one," he said finally. "A nylon line. A thin. Nylon. Line."

Kamran, at that point, had to have felt all eyes upon him and must have known he was supposed to react, so he looked at Matt, and he looked at the rest of us — his eyes going from one to another, meeting all of our impassive faces — and he shrugged with a jittery kind of laugh.

But Matt still hadn't reached his favorite part. On seeing Kamran's reaction, he glanced over at Gerry and, with a quick jerk of his head, exposed his broad Adam's apple and grinned. He did it with a cockiness, sure, but also with a delight — and I'm telling it to you straight when I say the guy is there for you. Wise-ass Gerry stepped right in. "So what happens then, Matt?" he said with this facetious eagerness. "Huh? Huh? Tell us, Matt! What happens?"

"Well, the instructor opens the door and leans out of the plane to see where in all of God's creation you are," Matt said. "She's hanging out there, looking and leaning, and everything on her begins to shake. Her lips shake," and here Matt stopped talking and with his fingers frenetically shook his own bottom lip, "her cheeks," his fingers moved to those areas and joggled as well, "even the folds of skin on her neck. At first I thought she was making faces at us — like, ha, isn't this funny? But that was only my brain messing with me because, really, it was the force of the wind. The eighty. Mile-an-hour. Winds. The ones you step into when it's your turn." Matt lifted his Pepsi to drink and as he did so he jerked back his head, and you just knew there was a wide smile behind the can.

Kamran said, "Oh, wow," shaking his head. Then he scratched the back of his neck — but I bet you there was no itch.

"Then what happens, Matt? C'mon, Matt, tell us the rest," Gerry said laughing, with his good-looking sly Irish face. Gerry's thirty-four, so when he laughs you can see the crow's feet.

"The instructor comes back in, out of the wind, and looks right at you," Matt said. "You're the first one she picks. She comes in close, you'd never figure she'd come so close, and she centers in, right into the middle of your eyes, hard, right into the depths of them and out the other side. And she says, 'Matt — you ready to jump?' You're thirty-two hundred feet in the air, you look down and everything you see looks like ants, the wind's hitting you at eighty miles an hour, and she asks you that. Right in your face." Here Matt leaned even further over the table toward Kamran, until he was only a nose's distance away.

"Kamran," he said. "You ready to jump?"

This is Matt's favorite part, and Kamran pulled back and

chuckled agitatedly, did just what was expected; and Matt and Gerry laughed out loud; and Lucy, Bob, and me broke into hyena smiles; and the routine, once again, was a success.

On the way back from Stan's, climbing up this incline single file on the cut-through back to our office, Gerry asked me if I wanted to go. He was right behind me in line and I could tell he was out of breath from the climb. I could hear his huffs between the words. "We're going again this Saturday, Pammy-Pam," he told me, "and there's plenty of room." As he asked, I swore I could feel his hot breath boring down my neck.

My instantaneous reaction was to stop climbing, wheel around, and gawk at him like he was crazy. But I didn't do this; I kept climbing, watching the placement of my feet self-consciously, trying not to think about a thing, trying not to listen. But I heard him say, "C'mon, Pam! C'mon, Pammy, Pammy, Pam. C'mon, Pamela," — egging me on. He sounded like a southern auctioneer with a pointy white goatee and a piece of rough rawhide tied around his neck: I have fifty, fifty, fifty — do I hear sixty?

To me, people who do this kind of thing are either whacko, unsatisfied-with-life thrill-seekers, or were once alien astronauts in some far and distant life. I'm none of these things. This is the kind of thing I would never do. Never in a million years. I don't even like Alpine skiing — and roller coasters are out of the question.

I waited until I had scaled the hill. I lagged a short way behind the group waiting for Gerry. "Pammy!" he said, coming up from behind, casting his hand down squarely on my shoulder, still out of breath. "What'll it be then, Pammy-Pam?"

When I look him in the eye, he is exactly my height; walking side-by-side we could balance a yard stick. I nodded my head almost imperceptibly, as if all this time it had been inevitable, and by now was some closed moot point. "I guess I'll go," I said. "Why not?"

Nathan, my brother, died in the spring. Four months ago. Scuba-diving off the Carolina coast during his college's spring break. His twenty-first birthday was coming up and we had a party planned. It was going to be a surprise. What else can I say? He was my only sibling.

At first I didn't do much. I showed up for work, ate dinner — alone or sometimes with my roommate — stayed in my room after that. Some time later, into the late spring and through the summer, I went and sat out on Matt and Gerry's back porch. People came over and we talked; they told stories and sometimes I laughed. I drank. When they left, Gerry went to bed, and Matt and I stayed on and talked. Matt would get me to talk about Nathan. He'd ask questions like: who was Nathan's favorite Celtic? Or, what did he think of rap? And as he'd ask, he'd look at me straight, like this was the way to go about it. And I'd talk. And that's it.

Later I went home and I thought about Nathan. And what I've come to realize is this: the nature of tragedy is not being ready. Death might not be so bad if you've lived for so long that your teeth all fall out. It might be like going to bed at the end of an iron-man triathlon — you've already swum two miles, biked a hundred, run twenty-six, and now, suddenly, the bed sheets look welcome.

But not before reaching twenty-one.

And I'm not ready to sky-dive, or bungee-cord jump from a hot-air balloon, or static line jump either. But I'm going. It's not that I want to die; I just want to experience not being ready. I just want to know what it feels like — what Nathan felt like — just as he began to eat water. Just as blue pressed in upon him. Just before he died.

It's passed around at work. Gerry tells Matt. Matt tells Lucy and Bob. Bob tells Kamran. Before I know it, six of us are going; and I'm the one who started the other three. Lucy wants to know what to wear, and Kamran wants to know if he can take pictures on the way down, and Bob wants to know if maybe he shouldn't drink anything, so when he gets on the plane he won't have to pee. They don't come to me with these things — they go straight to Gerry or Matt. But I become privy to the details. Soon, it's about all we discuss.

But there is one other thing we're beginning to discuss: the company's annual booze cruise is coming up this Friday night, the night before our excursion to Pepperell. It's advertised on the electronic invitations as a "sunset cruise overlooking Boston Harbor." But we know better; there's going to be a D.J. on board and plenty of alcoholic sustenance — hence the name "booze cruise."

Lucy wants to know what to wear for this event as well.

We're on the top deck of the ship and we're talking about superstition; the sun is just beginning to set. We've got a good night for it this year — nothing like last year when we were fogged in, and we couldn't even make out the planes zooming straight in over our heads. This year, the sun is turning all the right colors before it goes down.

Matt is smoking his Winston and saying, "It could very well be that if you think of something bad before it happens, it won't. I used to think that way as a kid, and every night before I went to sleep I'd think about all the bad things that could possibly happen the next day to prevent them." The breeze off the harbor flicks valleys through his hair, gently-rolling waves, and he tries to smooth them. "And you know," he says, "every single night I could always think of one more thing. You could never be finished with that kind of thing. Hell, if I was really vigilant about it, I never would've fallen asleep." He takes a gulp from his cup of draft beer.

"I like to think just the opposite," Lucy says. "I think — if you don't think about it, it won't happen." She reaches for Matt's cigarette, which he lets her have, then she taps the ashes off and inhales.

Matt thinks for a minute. "Could be," he says. "But my method worked for me. None of those bad things ever did happen."

"I know," Gerry says. "Let's do an experiment. Matt'll do it his way and think really bad things tonight, and, Lucy-Loose, you do it your way, and tomorrow we'll see who survives." Gerry is the only one who's laughing. Matt and I roll our eyes and Lucy does her disdainful look.

Then Bob, who hardly says a thing, pops up with, "Well, what are the fatality statistics on sky diving anyway?"

"You have the numbers on that, Gerry?" Matt says.

"Uh, I think it's something like thirty fatalities in any given year."

"That's nothing," Bob says. "In scuba diving it's around eight hundred." It's out before anybody can say a thing. Matt and Gerry give Bob these wicked looks that could melt steel, and Lucy touches my hand.

I shake it off, shake my head, shake Lucy's hand away, and drink some beer. Nathan used to joke that on the day he turned twenty-one he was going to buy six cases. All the beer he could carry in two arms. I don't think he ever found out that his birthday was going to fall on a Sunday, which, around here, means all the package stores are closed.

Gerry changes the subject. "Check out Amelia," he says. "She's like Saran Wrap — all over everybody except her intended, and transparent as hell." He does a little dance with his arched eyebrows and smirks lecherously.

We turn and look. Sure enough Amelia, who's engaged to Tony, has got an arm draped around Lawrence's neck. She looks to be whispering something in his ear — or she's got her tongue in it.

Earlier in the night, I spoke with Amelia. I asked her if she was getting any pre-nuptial jitters, since her wedding's coming up in a couple of weeks. I meant it facetiously, just making what I thought to be scintillating conversation. She said, "I throw up every night." At first I thought it was a joke, but she nodded her head, and, to convince me, pinched her eyebrows up tight.

Bob fumbles around in his shirt pocket for his cigarettes. He pulls one out and lights it, and as he does, I see the extra drink coupons he's somehow hoarded slide part way out. Gerry does too. "Hey, Bobby-Bob. How 'bout some coupons?" His hand is out firm and flat as a dried-up sea, and the next thing we know it's plastered with little gray squares.

Gerry and Matt go below to get a fresh round of beers with the drink coupons, and I remain up top with Bob and Lucy. When I look out at the horizon, only a thin line of maroon meets the sky. Stars are already coming out, and lights are being turned on in the high rises. It looks like infinite tic-tac-toe somehow — the irregular patterns of light gleaming like beacons from within the tall buildings. It looks like a game — but I realize I am powerless and can't play.

As soon as Matt and Gerry return, we leave the top deck, and the illuminating lighthouse on the horizon, and all of the stars, and we go down below to where the D.J.'s spinning. Gerry and I rattle and roll through a few tracks, then Lucy and Gerry, then Matt and me. In between I break for the bar to exchange some more drink coupons. On my second trip I find Amelia beside me. She's keeping herself erect via a bony white elbow perched on the bar, and her satiny brown hair is in her face. She looks at me through her hair. "Pam. I don't know what I'm going to do."

I usher her away from the bar, and we sit on one of the side benches built into the ship. She keeps brushing her hair up from out of her eyes and it keeps toppling back. She's got a gorgeous face like on a Greek statue: smooth straight nose, liquid hazelnut eyes — when you can see them — shapely crescents for lips. Her hair looks soft as silk tassels. She says, "Lately, Tony and I have been fighting all the time. About stupid things. I don't even know if I'm attracted to him anymore. And we've only got a week-and-a-half to go!" She's managing to keep her hair out of her face most of the time now, and when she looks at me her hazelnut eyes go M&M-melty.

Then she starts saying all the classic, confused, really stressed-out things: "What about my family and his family? We've got all the dresses. I'm not even one hundred per cent against it — fifty percent of me still thinks I should." She puts an arm around my shoulders and hugs me. It is a drunken hug, but still, I hug her back. "Sometimes, I think all I can do is wait 'till I get to the altar to say no," she tells me. She holds her supplicating face close, lifts her beseeching eyes to mine. It's apparent to me that she's waiting for advice, waiting on this ship that, like a lullaby, rocks its solemn way out to sea — but I'm not even married. Maybe that's the point.

"Well, I don't think you can go through with it, certainly," I tell her. "Not if you're not sure." I look around the deck to see who's listening. Then I turn back to Amelia, and with my eyes I try to sober her. "With this kind of thing," I tell her, "you have to be ready."

Tony, her intended, materializes out of the crew at the bar. He looks as if he's about to join us, or perhaps interrupt, but then he doesn't; he keeps going on his way. Amelia's arms are around me again and I'm holding her; the velvety quality of her hair is like goose down — like feathery tassels pressed flat against my chin.

I once held Nathan like that — held on for dear life. I don't remember what his hair felt like. That was the last time I ever really held him. We were playing in our backyard treehouse and the trap door became stuck. We couldn't get out and down to the ladder below, down to safety — except, somehow, Nathan could. Even though he was younger — nine to my almost-twelve — even though he was smaller, he climbed over the wall of the treehouse and, somehow, though he couldn't get to the ladder, made it down the tree. He told me to do the same, but I couldn't; I was never adventurous like Nathan. Our parents weren't home; it was Saturday — they were out doing errands. Nathan went to get the backyard hose, unscrewed it, and managed to throw it up to me. How high was that treehouse? I don't know. I tied the end around the railing of the treehouse wall. He told me to climb down. I told him I couldn't. He told me he'd catch me. I climbed over the edge, and slid part way down the hose. He caught me and I held on. He was smaller.

I remember feeling bad, being bigger and having him catch me. I remember thinking, that as we got older, there'd probably be plenty of times that I could help him. But now, I can't remember even one.

Saturday morning early, as planned, and we all have hangovers. The six of us are jam-packed into Gerry's mid-size sedan. Gerry's driving, and I'm in the back seat feeling like I might puke, and we're on our way to the inevitable. We had to leave by seven this morning so we can get there by eight-thirty, since, first, us novices have to sit though training school.

Lucy, for the occasion, has settled on tight clothing. Everything on her clings — her pants, her tanktop, even her sweatshirt — as if she's afraid if anything came loose it might catch in her line, or get caught in the wind and pull her away. Kamran brought his camera after all — not for his own flight down, but for after he lands to snap others. Bob's as quiet as usual; and I'm just trying to hold down the green bile that's been threatening to shoot up every mile of the way. We stop at a rest room and Matt hands out aspirin.

"I don't feel so swell," I tell people. I tell everybody. Most of them look as chartreuse as me. Kamran's chipper though; I believe he drank soda water last night. He's walking around the rest area blabbing his head off. I think it must be nerves. "How many seconds does it last in all?" he asks. "When I land, what do I do with my feet? Am I arching right?" He's got his head tipped back and his arms flung out and his feet spread firmly out in the grass. He looks a little like one of those adventurers on the T.V. show "Intrepid Explorers". But the hyped-out pitch of his voice doesn't do much to calm me.

For the last leg of the journey, and on request, I get the front seat. I'm yawning a lot; I'm yawning continuously — it's a habit I have when I'm nervous. I'm yawning, and trying to breathe regularly, and looking straight out in front of me at the quickly-disappearing lines in the road, when Matt, who's sitting beside me, says, "What do you call six blondes in a row?" He nudges my arm.

"What?" Gerry asks.

"A wind tunnel." I've heard it before, but I know Matt's only trying to cheer me.

"I've got one," Gerry says. He looks in the rearview mirror to make sure his audience is alert. "What do you call a thousand lawyers sunk to the bottom of the ocean?" No-one says anything. "A good start."

I've heard that one before, too, but Kamran howls. His laugh dies down to a wheeze, and all you can hear for the next mile-and-a-half is his irregular nasal snort.

Nathan used to make me laugh. On long car rides late at night, driving home from Florida or Virginia, we'd both get silly. We'd be sitting way in the back seat in one of the luxurious Buicks my parents always had. We'd get tired of playing twenty questions, or hangman, or of guessing the capitals of states. The time would come when we'd both just know we were going to lose it. Nathan could say anything then, like, "Pam, Bickford's!" or, "Pam, Sunoco!" pointing out the places we'd pass. And I'd just die laughing — and so would he.

Sometimes I'd tease him. "You could be a comedian," I'd say hysterically, like I could never imagine anything so funny, and I'd point at him like it was a riot. Of course I was joking; nothing he ever said — Bickford's, Sunoco — was really that funny.

You could be a fireman, Nathan. You could be an astronaut. You could be...

It's a clear day at least, a clear day in September, which I know I should be thankful for, but maybe if it wasn't I wouldn't have to go.

"I just know I'm going to have to piss," Bob says finally from the back seat. "I just know, no matter how many times I piss first, when I get on the plane I'm going to have to piss again."

I can hear Lucy smoothing down her already-skin-tight pants in the back seat. "I brought Chap Stick, Pam. For the wind burn," she informs me.

This is all becoming a little too surreal. I don't respond, and Gerry takes a hand off the wheel and elbows me. "Wake up, Pammy-Pam."

I feel like a major-league zombie and I don't care. My face, by now, must be green-gray, and I just keep staring straight out in front of me, not moving my head to look at anyone. I can only imagine my expression is heavy-lidded, serious, doomed. My mouth is part-way open, my lips are dry, and I barely remember to breathe. I am well past the yawning stage now; I am about ready to jump from my skin. To pass out. To run. I don't even like to fly; I'm one of those kinds who get motion sick — like when I'm hungover and I ride in a car.

Matt starts in. I almost can't believe it. "You're strapped into your thirty pound 'chute. You're thirty-two hundred feet up, you're traveling at eighty miles an hour, and the wind is roaring. When you look down, the treetops look like moss. Barely discernible. Extremely minuscule. Moss."

Kamran's chuckling nervously and Lucy's patting down her pants. Bob is quiet again as always.

"All that's connecting you with the rest of your days ahead is a line. A line. A thin. Nylon," — Lucy and Kamran join in for the rest — "line," they say together in unison. Laughter fills the car — excitable twitters, Kamran's wheeze.

I wish Matt hadn't started in because now I can't stop it from playing in my head. I see blue — weightless, diaphanous blue — and I'm falling through it. I can't slow down, it's too late, and it's terrible. Something has pushed me, and now that I'm falling I realize it's a mistake. I see blue; I'm engulfed in blue. Blue sky. Blue sea.

"The instructor steps in from the wind," Matt says, "her neck folds still flapping. She puts her face right up to yours, and it's as if you're seeing her pores through a microscope. You hear nothing — but the booming of your heart." Matt pauses for a moment, then I hear him turn toward me, practically springing in his seat. From my frozen peripheral vision I can see his face, looming. "Pam," he says, "you ready to jump?!"

The car is quiet, and then suddenly everything becomes acute as a result. Matt's window is part way open and I can hear us zooming past the telephone poles on the highway. There's an interruption in the sound every time we pass one, and then the interruptions get further and further apart. People are waiting for my answer; Lucy's no longer patting down anything, and Gerry's stopped making jokes. I look at Matt.

"No," I say, "I guess I'm not."

There's silence in the car at first, until finally Gerry snickers through his nose — a sharp definitive hiss of air. He snickers again, and this time sounds join from his throat. But no one else joins in.

"No, I mean it," I say.

Gerry turns to look at me, and I hear Kamran, Bob, and Lucy lean forward in the back seat. "I'm just not ready," I say. "What's the point if I'm not ready?"

I don't turn to read their expressions, so I don't know what they're thinking now. But it doesn't matter; I'm thinking myself. I'm thinking about this thing, and about how it isn't the kind of thing you just go ahead with — not when you have a choice. And I'm thinking about Nathan — and how that's the difference between him and me.

Finally, I turn to look at Matt, to see how I'm doing, to judge the effect this all has. His face is blank as a chalkboard, blank as the smoothest cement on a wall. Because he's not grinning, I can't even see his Adam's apple. I'm thinking now about how the rest of the car is so quiet; and, as we take the turn and pull our car onto the drive, I'm thinking — I don't care how close the instructor's face comes to mine.

Blues

Ray Davis

She'd had to come home early again, even though it meant missing the Saturday night tips. She splashed water on her eyes at the kitchen sink, wiped her hands on the dish-towel, and let her face dry in the air.

The wardrobe was still open from this morning. She left it open now, after changing clothes and shoes. But the door would get shut sometime, so Simone Simon had to be trained not to hide there. "Come on, haven't you heard of Stonewall?" she chided. She lifted a black slipper from under the cat to dislodge it and then to entice it out. "Monster," she said affectionately, picking it up.

She sat on the couch. It was seven; there was a lot of time to kill. A good chance to sketch out ideas for the group show at BroadGall. It was coming up soon.

She couldn't.

She should have asked around work for some barbiturates, although it was a little dangerous with all the booze left in the apartment.

She turned on the cheap one-piece stereo that her sister had loaned her, kneeled before the squat column of milk crates, and dragged her fingertips across the records.

Simone Simon paced behind her a few times, impersonally leaning into her ratty jeans as though caught by her gravitational pull. She stood up and opened the shoebox on top, full of cassettes. She tried a Killing Joke compilation but snatched it out after less than a minute. A tape labeled 'BRAHMS SYMP.' followed the same path.

Finally she turned to the radio, stopping at a college station playing a modern percussion piece. She adjusted the plastic-coated wires which curled from the back of the stereo but they didn't improve the signal.

She thought of the leftover pizza in the fridge, its stale crust and its oils curdled, and her stomach turned, but partly from hunger, she knew. If she didn't eat, she would be awake all night, and she needed sleep.

As the microwave sang, she forked out Simone Simon's dinner. She hadn't wanted the microwave; his parents had given it to him. She probably got it because she was "the cook in the family." Amazing the number of things she didn't want which had been left. She bumped into new ones all the time, looking for things which were gone. Simone Simon's dry food looked fine but she topped it off anyway.

She dabbed the excess grease from the pizza with a napkin. There was no parmesan left, so she used salt to coarsen the bland glistening surface. With the pizza, she drank cold red wine from a tumbler of thick greenish glass. She was maybe two-thirds down the bottle and it was still surprisingly potable. The cork would probably fall apart long before the wine did.

She turned the radio off.

As she washed her glass and plate, a thought came to her. She herself didn't think it, and this sense of an intrusive voice attracted her attention pleasantly, like Clifton Webb's or Marlene Dietrich's first scene in a movie, wrecking the established mood ten minutes after their names appear in the titles.

For some years after adolescence, she had occasionally felt a similar impetus. Although it had led her into mistakes, she'd valued it and missed it as it appeared less often. She associated its loss with an odd memory:

In a grad student's narrow bed one morning, too soon after a night of smoke and braggadocio, trying not to wake the neighboring body as she shifted, she felt and saw her soul leave. It was light blue; it fled, impossibly fast, toward the closed bedroom door and vanished into it. Her consciousness remained intact and panicky in the bed, but something it considered a soul had been stripped or extracted.

As her tearing eyes focused on the streak left on the door, she saw it was the grad student's faded jeans, hanging there by a belt loop. It had been raining heavily; the jeans had gotten soaked coming to the room and they were drying.

When she read about selling one's soul, or trapping a soul in a camera (so easy for her to imagine: the mad dash through the lens, then the click, shutting off the escape route), or even the probability of the soul's existence, she thought of that morning, but never felt it appropriate to bring up. She didn't know what attitude to take.

The voices left to her afterwards were not distinguished by tone or personality. They were like those overdubbed demo tapes assembled by the shy, budget-conscious, or simply difficult, run only by the need to keep silence at arm's length, to fill in certain parts left empty, like conversation at a bad party.

Now she went to the swaybacked wardrobe that she and he had bought, assembled, shifted, and constantly prodded back into wobbling shape. Simone Simon darted out as she reached in.

Typically, thoughtlessly, he'd forgotten to take his bathrobe. Last week, she'd tossed some of her winter clothes in front of it on the shelf, to hide it. She spread them apart and pulled the robe down.

She held it by the arms. The pits were slightly whitened, probably from bleach. It still gave off his tenacious acidy smell. She'd worn the robe to bed when he was away. Against the light, she saw some thin spots and a hole at one shoulder. She began tearing there.

Almost immediately, a rough fingernail caught in the cloth, tugging out a loop of thread. She freed it, chewed it smooth, and continued.

When about halfway down the back, she stopped and found a pair of long scissors to help undo the seams. Once a few threads were cut, they seemed to come apart quickly, as if split by an axe. Sleeves, suddenly drapelike, dropped to the floor.

The hems and belt loops were harder.

She spread the torn terrycloth over the floor, studied it, rearranged it, studying again, like a seer over tea leaves or entrails.

She moved the smaller pieces quickly out of the way onto the massive bureau, knocking a tiny bottle or two over into the sea of paper already there, then brought them back down one by one, fitting them together. Simone Simon insisted on batting the edges, which was a nuisance.

It looked like an approximated oval, like a diamond with a short attention span.

In the same drawer as the scissors was a ball of jute twine left from Christmas mailings. She retrieved it and then rummaged through her gray-and-blue plastic sewing box, sorting past crochet and knitting needles to a cream-colored yarn needle.

After bending the twine into the needle's wide eye, she roughly stitched the larger pieces together. This was mostly for show; she secured the trickier junctures with a light blue thread, invisible against the robe's material. Sags and gaps would be acceptable, and she could add more support tomorrow.

It was very late and she still didn't know what she was to do with it. She pictured a Frankenstein kite over New York Bay, twine, wrapped around her and under her arms, suspending her between the blue wing and the gray water. It would be visible from the Staten Island ferry. She laughed and waited for more word.

When it came, she nodded. She lay down on the cloth, too tall to fit until she curled into her usual sleeping position. She noted pressure points and tried to form an image of herself, lying there, viewed from above.

She disarmed the smoke alarm next to the door, jumping at its death-yelp. "Surprised you too, I bet," she told Simone Simon. In the kitchen, she collected a few boxes of matches and moistened the dish-towel, just in case.

She tested a lighted match on one of the leftover scraps of robe. The edges glowed and snuffed: it was flame-retardant.

She scorched the cloth at the places she'd pressed most sharply and at extremities. Match heads and black and gray charcoals were used to roughen these points to lines, partly stippled, partly streaked, until the cloth held a study half skeletal, half silhouetted; a surface ambiguously blasted against or burnt through.

She turned out the light, stripped and made her way to the couch about five in the morning. She felt somehow observed, but still slept deeply. Soon after waking, lying under a light sheet, left hand dangling down to the cushions on the floor, she dreamt:

She stood on a skirt of rough sand before a cliff of yellowish stone. In front of her, rocks and shells, increasing in size, straggled into the darkening ocean. The sun was white and fairly high, casting her shadow back onto the cliff, which in turn reflected white light onto her back. Sea spray continuously covered her and continuously evaporated in the heat, powdering her body with soft white salt. Her sweat cooled under the thickening powder. She closed her eyes and the lids were covered as well. She became radiant, and the sun came down to her.

She showered and shampooed, threw on some light clothes, and went out for the *Times* and breakfast. She'd slept late and there was a long line, but the customers took it well in the mild weather. The guy behind the counter slipped her a free bagel and she ended up with three, two for the freezer.

Back home, she made a mug of strong oily coffee and drank it with her bagel. After she was done, she gave the excess baked salmon salad to Simone Simon. She went to the piece she'd made last night and looked down at it, hands hooked behind her neck.

Then she bent to the cloth and rolled it tightly, walking forward. She folded the roll into thirds, carried it into the kitchen, and pushed it into the tall plastic garbage can. It almost filled the bag; there was just room for the coffee grounds and newspaper.

I asked her why.

"Sorry," she said. "I hate autobiographical art."

Dances with Death

Stan Shursky

It's funny. It's a major, joyous, holiday weekend. You haven't seen your cousin in a couple of years and your brothers since last Christmas. Everybody's happy. You are sitting around drinking a few beers shooting the bull on a brilliant sunny day, laughing. The sun is reflected so bright off the snow you can't look at it. So, what do you talk about? Why, you talk about death, of course.

A discussion about death is never started by someone saying, "Hey, let's talk about death. It'll be a real blast!" You kind of sneak up on it. It probably starts with someone saying they nearly had a car accident on the way over. Then someone tells a story where they experienced some level of danger and walked away. Then someone else tells how close they came to dying then everybody jumps in with their near-death experiences.

It started by swapping car accident stories. Everybody has at least one. Some guy runs a stop sign and you have to make some creative marks on the pavement to avoid him. A split-second different and somebody would have been seriously hurt. Everybody has one. Especially if they drive in Massachusetts. When it was my turn as the speaker as we went around the circle, I told the story about fast driving in the old Jag.

It was the summer after I got my bachelor's degree. I was living in the frat house and working at the Draper Lab. In the summer we rented rooms to any and all comers to make some money. There were a couple of girls living there. I was hanging out with Moira.

I come home from a day at the Draper Lab and I am ready to drop because Moira and I didn't do much sleeping the night before, if you get my drift. I am ready for a serious nap and they all jump me at once. Paul, Moira, Doug and his girlfriend. They want to go fast driving around Spot Pond in Stoneham. Well, I am dead tired. I try to beg off with the excuse that I am too tired but finally they goad me into it.

Off we go. Paul in his Alfa, Doug in his Triumph GT-6 and me in the old Jag. We got to Stoneham and get going around Spot Pond in the dark. It is a real nice circuit. Two lanes with a median almost all the way around. And lotsa curves! We are having a grand time! No top, wind in our hair. We are squealing our tires through the turns, passing all the slow drivers left and right.

We are on the third time around and I am so tired my concentration is starting to drift, you know? I am thinking that this time around is the last pass. When I stop thinking and re-focus on the road, I notice that I am going straight and the road is headed off to the left. Ha, ha, ha. Well, I bang the gearshift down into third, hit the brakes and I am steering hard left. I am trying to guess if I am going to make this turn and doing my level best to try to keep the back end of the car from beating the front end around the corner, when there is a scream in my ear and Moira grabs my arm! Ha, ha, ha! You wish you could be really cool and say something like: "Pardon me. I am trying to save our lives here. Could you please release my arm. I am using it." But it comes out more like: "Gawdammit. Leggo my arm!" Ha, ha, ha!

Anyway, I ignore her arm and use my strength to overcome any interference. We drift from the inside lane all the way to the outside lane. I swear my tires nearly clipped the curb on the far side of the road.

Ha, ha, ha.

Everybody has a good chuckle and the speaker position continues around the circle. When the speaker role comes around again I decide it is time to escalate and stop telling car stories. I decide to tell my golf-course story. I figured I'd save the good ones for later. It was one of my milder near-death experiences.

I remember the summer during high school when I was working at Tarry Brae Golf Course. It was a warm sunny day. The kind of day when working outside is wonderful. You get a farmer's tan. A good tan on your arms and face but because of Course rules you can't take your shirt off and tan your chest and back. It was the kind of day when death is as far from your mind as anything could be.

It was almost quitting time. We were rushing around to get everything cleaned up in time to leave on time. Isn't that always the way? You are in a rush so you aren't quite as careful as you should be. We were out on the sixth fairway in the woods cutting trees. We had felled several large maples and a yellow birch. We would have been done sooner but the bozo running the chainsaw used it to try to cut granite and we had to get the chain sharpened. Well, we had the trees cut into pieces and were trying to get all the wood dumped back by the equipment barn.

We had cut the boles into two-foot lengths and loaded them in the Toro tractor with the dump body. You know what a Toro tractor looks like, right? They still make them but it looks like a 1930's design. They are really nothing more than something like a pickup truck frame with a louvered hood like a 1930's car. They have a utilitarian dash with a couple of gauges, three pedals and a shift lever, and a steering wheel to point it in the right direction. They have a single seat behind the wheel and the tires are open to the air, dual wheels on the back. No windshield, no doors, no roof, not even a running board. Just an engine in front and the dump body behind.

Behind the driver's seat they have this dump body. It isn't very big and the lift system is manually operated. All it really is is a pivot pin. If you loaded your load too far forward you couldn't dump it unless you released the catch, revved it up and popped the clutch. That was always a blast!

Like I said, it was getting towards quitting time and I was rushing. We loaded the dump body full and I was heading back to the equipment barn to dump it. Remember, from the sixth fairway you come up past the club house and then go down the driveway and cross the road to the barn? Remember how the driveway is a long, relatively steep hill? Well, those Toros are geared so low that you couldn't go very fast and I was in a rush. I had it in fourth gear and at the top of the hill I wound it out to top speed and pushed in the clutch so I was really winging going down the driveway. It was great! The wind in your hair. The sun on your face. You are watching the ground whizz by your feet. Death is sitting at your shoulder. You just don't realize it.

When I got to the bottom and had to cross the road I engaged the clutch to slow down. It was then I learned that you shouldn't load those dump bodies so full. That's what happens when you are in a rush. Well, the logs were higher than the top of the dump body. So when I slowed down the top log slid forward. It went right past my left shoulder and out of the corner of my eye I could see it drop under the left set of dual wheels. You know that sinking feeling you have watching something like that happen in slow motion? Well, I had it! You have a split second to realize you are in trouble and you have to react. That was exciting! Those Toros have no springs to speak of and the log was about six inches in diameter. Ha, ha, ha! Well, when the duals hit that baby it was like trying to ride a bucking bronco. Ha, ha, ha! There were logs flying everywhere and I was just able to hang on and bring the Toro to a stop. There were logs rolling all over the road. Lucky there were no cars coming! Ha, ha, ha. There I was running around like a mad man in the middle of the road, looking to see if anybody was watching, pitching the logs back in the dump body as fast as I could. Ha, ha, ha!

But you know, if I wasn't holding on to the steering wheel with both hands or if one of the logs caught me in the back of the head, I would have fallen under those rear duals and been a road waffle. Then we all got a little somber for a minute. The speaker's role passed on.

Now it was Cliff's turn to tell a story. He told the one about the time he was working with my father in the woods. He was carrying a running chainsaw over to the next tree to cut the limbs off. Those big old heavy chainsaws were something. They weren't nearly as safe, if you can ever call a chainsaw safe, as they are today. The trigger control had a lock so you could lock it full on when you were cutting down a really big tree. Well, Cliff tripped! Ha, ha, ha! In falling his hand twisted just right to lock the chainsaw on at maximum. Ha, ha, ha! And he landed in a pushup position with the chainsaw blade whizzing by his face. Ha, ha, ha! One good thing about working in the woods, you get strong arms. Cliff was able to throw himself aside to safety. Ha, ha, ha, what a blast!

Nobody else had a story so it was my turn again. It looked like Cliff and I were going to be swapping tales to see who had the best.

Remember, that summer at Monticello Blacktop? Boy, that was a dangerous place to work. Huh? You know, I had a humorous little escapade my first week of work there. Remember that old beatup Dodge dump truck? That thing couldn't haul itself out of the gravel pit much less haul a load of gravel. It had that faulty tailgate latch, remember. The first day I was there Joe told me when I released the tailgate I gotta check the latch to make sure it had released before I raised the body and dumped the load.

Well, I was running gravel up out of the pit and dumping it in the hopper for the crusher. Of course, that old Dodge gets a case of the hiccups or something. By the time we get it going again the crusher is on empty and I am dashing back and forth from pit to hopper as fast as I can go, you know? I'm playing catch-up. I am jammin' the gears as I come hammering up the hill from the pit. Ha, ha, ha! I forget about the damn tailgate latch. I back the truck up to the hopper, release the tailgate, slam the dump into gear and gun the engine. Ha, ha, ha! Well, the body goes up until it gets high enough so all the gravel slides back. Naturally, the latch hasn't fully released so there is only about a ten inch gap between the tailgate and the body. Ha, ha, ha! The gravel hits the tailgate and has nowhere to go. I am sitting there with the door open and my left leg hanging out because I had just released the latch. Ha, ha, ha. Anyway, when the gravel hits the tailgate the front wheels of the truck come up off the ground. Ha, ha, ha! And they keep coming! Ha, ha, ha! They get about three feet off the ground. Here I am staring up at the morning sun and I am about ready to piss my pants when the gravel leaking out that ten inch gap catches up and the truck slowly settles back to earth again. Ha, ha ha! I bet that would have impressed the foreman. First week on the job and I almost had the dump truck lying on its back in the crusher hopper. Ha, ha, ha!

Hey, remember how I used to grease that crusher and the separator screens. I would run up those rubber conveyor belts with a grease gun in each hand. That was a blast! It was a lot faster than climbing up the stupid ladders. The rollers were three feet apart, just about my uphill stride. I must have been about fifty feet off the ground when I got to the top. Great view! Ha, ha, ha! That was fun. You just didn't look down when you ran up. That was the trick!

And when that huge Euclid bucket loader kept blowing O-rings in the hydraulic system. You know how I used to change those? We always needed the damn loader all the time so it could never be down for a minute. If one of those two loaders was down the other one just couldn't do everything.

You'll love this! Ha, ha, ha! I'd pull the loader in the garage and get under it on the creeper. Ha, ha, ha! Then I would loosen the two bolts holding the fitting with the O-ring. Then, get this, I would hold the fitting with my right hand and with my left I would push a piece of cardboard between my face and old oil drum. Ha, ha, ha! Then I would pull the fitting loose and the four-hundred-degree hydraulic fluid would run down the cardboard into the drum instead of in my face. Ha, ha, ha. I'd pop in a new O-ring, bolt'er up, fill'er up and give'er back to you ready to roll. Ha, ha, ha. Fifteen minutes! Max! Ha, ha, ha!

Oh, God! Remember what happened to poor Gene? That silly fool had to change the bucket pins in the bucket loader. Remember he stood the bucket on its teeth? God, he should have known better. He replaced the pins that connected the hydraulic rams. That was OK because the arms were still supporting and balancing the bucket.

Then he took the old pins out of the arms. He took both of them out! It would probably have been OK if he only took one out. God, there was nothing keeping the bucket standing on its teeth except good luck. He was just about to put in the new pins, remember. He was trying to line up the pins in the holes, but the pins come through the arms from the inside. He had his body between the ram and the bucket arm. If that bucket had kicked out a few seconds earlier, the ram coming down would have cut him in half. That may have been better than what happened. The ram caught him by the head against the bucket arm. Right along the jaw.

I remember when I came running over. He was hanging there caught by his head with blood leaking out of his ears. God, I remember we couldn't figure out how to get him out of there. I had to climb up in the loader and I couldn't see what was going on. They were telling me to move things around with Gene hanging there by his head! It sure gave me a case of the willies, I'll tell you. Finally, they figured out how to free him and they let him down and I could get down out of the loader.

Remember how long we waited for the ambulance? I thought it would never come. I clocked it. It was twenty minutes. Longest twenty minutes in my life! Remember he stopped breathing while we were waiting? God, I thought he was dead, but then he started breathing again. I remember how helpless I felt waiting for that stupid ambulance. Then when the ambulance came we had to get Gene out from under the loader. We couldn't move the loader because the bucket wasn't attached. Gene was a pretty big man and the EMTs needed help. Everybody just stood there like their shoes were nailed to the floor. Cliff and I had help the EMTs and I'm not real good around blood, you know? We got him out and in the ambulance. Last I heard Gene was in a wheelchair and pretty much a vegetable. When something like that happens, you always wonder what you could have done differently that might have helped him. God, if he had just been more careful!

Then we all got thoughtful. At one time or another Vince, Cliff and I had all worked at the Monticello Blacktop plant. Instead of Gene it could have been any of us that made that dumb mistake. Cliff and I had been there and seen it first-hand. The others had a pretty grim mental picture dancing in front of them.

Finally, Cliff perks up and tells another logging story. He was in the woods and had parked the bulldozer on a slope and was hammering the hooks into a couple of logs to pull them out of the woods. He had one log attached and is pounding on the other when the bulldozer takes it in its head to head down the hill. Bulldozers are pretty heavy and aren't likely to take off like that. Well, Cliff was dancing around trying to get his feet out of the logs which were following the bulldozer, you know? Anyway, he gets clear, runs up alongside the bulldozer, vaults aboard and has just gotten his ass in the seat, ha ha ha, when the bulldozer hits a rock with deep roots. The bulldozer pitches him out of the seat, right up over the blade and he lands in front of the thing! Ha, ha, ha. Well, good thing the rock stopped the bulldozer or Cliff would have been a mess. Ha, ha, ha.

After the laughter had subsided I decided to tell my kicker near-death escapade.

You know, if you really want to talk about staring down death, you gotta get a good look at him. These stories we were telling were over before we knew it. Death glanced our way but he wasn't interested in us. I am talking about looking him square in the face and seeing the blackness of his empty eye sockets. I mean staring him down and saying: "Not today! You can't have me today!" Have you ever done that? Well, I have.

If I had to choose a way I didn't want to die, it would either be fire or water. Fire is much too painful and water is too slow. With water you get several minutes after your lungs fill up with burning seawater to face death one on one.

This is a story from my days down in Newport, RI. My friend Bob was down for the weekend. It's amazing how many friends visit when you live near the beach! Anyway, Bob was down and we decided to go to the beach. Lovely day. I decided to take him to Reject Beach. You know the swatch of public sand near Bailey's Beach?

We were having a grand time. The sun was shining and all the locals were there including the semi-famous Four Sisters. They were a family of four sisters that had more than their share of cuteness genes. We were tanning ourselves waiting for the tide to go out, you know. In Rhode Island the law says any sand below the high tide mark is public. So when the tide goes out we can walk across Bailey's Beach past the very private Spouting Rock Beach Club to Spouting Rock.

While we were waiting, this girl was leaving the beach and she was trying to put on a t-shirt and take off her wet bikini top. She got them crossed up, you know? So she has nothing on. I'm looking right at her and she is looking right at me so I give her my best shit-eating grin, you know? I told Bob but he said he missed it. So I offered to go ask her to do it again. He says 'sure', but I declined. Ha, ha, ha.

Anyway, the tide got part of the way out so I offered to show Bob Spouting Rock. We walked over the beach and up on the rocks to Spouting Rock. Well that sucker was really humming, I'll tell you. You gotta picture this. Spouting Rock is a small cave in the rocks at water level. When a wave comes along, the wave goes into the cave, hits the back and splashes out. It used to really spout but the property owner got so tired of people coming across his land to get to the rock that he dynamited it. So now it isn't nearly as good as it used to be.

The really fun part of Spouting Rock is the channel in front of the cave. The mouth of the cave is narrow, only a couple of feet wide. The channel in front is shaped like a funnel so the wave gets funneled into the cave and amplified about three times in height. What we used to do was play in the channel. You would get sucked toward the cave on the in stroke and then you shoot out the channel on the exhaust stroke. It was great fun.

And it was really running that day. The water depth in the cave mouth was about four or four and a half feet, about chest high. But when the cave emptied it literally emptied. I mean the gravel at the mouth of the cave was rattling around. The waves were in perfect harmony with the cave. After it emptied another wave would come slamming into the cave. It would fill the mouth almost full which must be about ten feet high. KAWOOSH! And the water would come splashing out and then it would empty again. Like I said, I never saw anything like it! Truly impressive! The story around town is that several people have died in there over the years.

So we were having fun shooting down the channel on the outflow from the cave. We were having a great time. The Cannonball was there. I don't know the guy's name, but he is really round and a great swimmer. He would go in the cave and come shooting out like the guy that gets shot out of the cannon in the Circus. He would just keep doing it, over and over. I had to admire him because I can't swim all that well. I am just a splasher, you know?

Well, we had been splashing around for the better part of an hour when Bob and I took a rest. We were just sitting on the rocks by the channel watching a couple of kids, couldn't have been more than about eleven, playing in the channel and the Cannonball shooting out of the cave over and over. We were just sitting there soaking up the nice hot sun when we realize the kids are kinda screaming for help. They were tired and what with Spouting Rock running like a runaway freight train, they were in trouble. I grabbed the nearest one's hand and pulled him out. Bob jumped in the channel and pushed the other one out on the rocks by his ass. Both of them sat on the rocks like a couple of drowned rats. Ha, ha, ha. They were real glad we fished them out. We sat back down figuring we had done our good deed for the day. We had saved a couple of kids from drowning. I should have known then that Death was lurking in the area but I wasn't paying attention.

After a little while we wanted to play in the channel again but it was dead, flat calm. I mean the water was hardly even lapping the rocks, you know. So I told Bob I was going in the cave. He tried to talk me out of it. But I was in the mouth of the cave standing there in chest-deep water and in a happy-go-lucky mood and I just headed in the cave. The cave was really nice. It takes a gentle curve to the right as it goes back. The sun was shining off the water and the reflected spots of sun were dancing on the roof of the cave. Real pretty. The floor comes up and the roof comes down so they meet in the back. I could see why the water comes shooting out. When it comes pounding in the cave it gets to the back and has nowhere to go so it follows the curve of the roof up and out.

I got around the curve and there was the Cannonball standing in ankle deep water at the very back of the cave. I was about three quarters of the way in and the water was just above my knees. I said "hello" to the Cannonball and he said "hi" back. Then he asked me if I had ever been in there before. I told him no. He said something like, "You mean you have never done this before?" And he sounds a little incredulous, you know? So I said no. As we were talking, I noticed that the water that was above my knees had dropped to my ankles. I hear the gravel rattling a little. Just then the Cannonball shouts, "Here it comes!" I was looking towards the back of the cave at him and in my right ear I heard something that sounded like a freight train coming into the cave. I whipped around to the right and there was this wall of water coming down the cave! My first thought was a very calm, "Holy shit!". Well, I sucked onto the cave wall and tried to pretend I was a barnacle. It was a good thing I was on the inside of the curve. If I was on the outside of the curve I would have been splatted on the back wall like a fly under a flyswatter.

The incoming wave knocked me off my feet and dinged me on the floor of the cave a couple of times. The wave hit the back wall with a clap like thunder in that enclosed space. The water went shooting by me going the other way along the roof. Then the whole cave was just one mass of sloshing water and foam. In seawater the human body has buoyancy and floats. It isn't the same with foam. You don't float at all and you can't breathe it. I know, I tried. Ha, ha, ha.

So there I was with seawater in my lungs and I was doing my absolute level best to get the hell out of the mouth of the cave. I couldn't see a thing because of all of the foam. I was just heading toward the light. Well, the cave starts to empty and I get sucked along like crazy. I am really glad, you know, because everything is going my way: out! The cave empties and I hear the gravel rattling like a son of a gun out in the mouth of the cave but I haven't made much headway because I was originally carried back into the cave, you know?

The gravel stops rattling and another wave comes roaring in. I was not far enough out to brace across the walls. It was too wide inside. So I dug my toes into the gravel on the cave floor and tried to grab a crack in the rock wall but it didn't matter. I took a second wave on the chin and got thrown back into the cave. There was another KABOOM as the wave hit the back wall and another KAWOOSH as the water went screaming by overhead. By now there was no blood in my veins. It was all pure, unadulterated adrenalin. My heart was pounding like crazy. You might say I experienced complete terror, but I wasn't going to let death take me without a struggle.

This time I was struggling not to breathe foam and I was swimming with all I had for the cave mouth. The water exhausted from the cave and I was closer to the mouth, miraculously. But I knew I was going to have to take another wave because the gravel was rattling like Death's chains and I was getting pretty tired. A third wave came pounding in. KABOOM! KAWOOSH! I fought like it is the very last thing I was ever going to do. Which was probably pretty close to true. Ha, ha, ha. When the water cleared out I was standing in the mouth of the cave looking out. It was a grand sight! But right in front of me was another wave building in the channel. It was screaming down on me. The gravel was rattling around my ankles. As the wave neared me it was getting higher and higher as the channel got narrower and narrower. I was staring up at a wall of water totally exhausted. I knew I had to take another hit.

I braced myself kittycorner across the cave opening and the water hit me like a Mack truck. I was splatted on the rock like a bug on your car windshield. The water rushed around me forcing its way into the cave. There was no way, having gotten this far out, that I was going back into the cave. I braced myself with everything I had and hung on. Water went by me and went KABOOM! KAWOOSH! Water came shooting out over my head. Ha, ha, ha. The cave started to empty and I felt a hand right between my shoulder blades. It was the Cannonball! I had completely forgotten about him. He gave me a shove from behind and the water comes shooting out of the cave and I popped out of there like a champagne cork. I went shooting down the channel with tons of water behind me. I couldn't do a thing because I was pretty much exhausted but I could see Bob along the channel holding out a hand for me to catch. I just barely grabbed it and he pulls me from the water. Ha, ha, ha! Actually, whenever Bob told the story he swore I leapt up out of the water and grabbed his wrist like a vise. Ha, ha, ha. It sure didn't feel like that to me. Ha, ha, ha.

Afterwards, for fifteen minutes I stood on the rocks unable to move. I was quaking from the cool water and fear. But the funny part, ha, ha, ha, was, I was a total mess. I was bleeding from everywhere. The barnacles had sliced my hands, I had no calluses left on my hands, I'll tell you. I had scrapes on my legs, arms, chest. Everywhere! Ha, ha, ha. So now I am the one looking like a bloody, drowned, shivering rat. Ha, ha, ha! I was a real sight. Ha, ha, ha! And boy does that salt water sting! Ha, ha, ha!

Everybody in the room is staring at me. Just staring. That is my best near-death experience. It IS a crowd stopper. We all take a swig of beer and relax.

Here's the really funny part. When we are all quiet for a little while, my mother pokes her head around the corner of the wall and says, "How come I never heard any of these stories before?" We all start laughing and I shoot back, "We didn't think you would really want to!"

I don't know why talking about death is so much fun. Maybe it's a way of thanking God that you are alive. Maybe it's a release from some of the memories that are a little too black to face easily on any other day than a beautiful day. Like poor Gene who didn't quite escape. Maybe it's just bragging and one-upmanship-style camaraderie.

You can look death in the eye too often. We all know that. One day you won't walk away. But today is not that day.

A Trip Out West

Sara Berkeley

To get to his own front door, Hughie had to move eleven boxes of garden refuse. The hedge clippings had dried to skeletal sticks and the leaves underfoot crumpled scratchily when he trod on them. Hughie was a big man and that summer he had not been playing much tennis. He breathed heavily as he hauled the boxes up the short steep drive; he began to perspire and he was muttering to himself.

To open the door he had to fidget with the immense bunch of keys Kate had collected over 30 years. Some of these keys probably didn't open anything anywhere. They might have belonged to wardrobes Kate had sold to jumble sales, or to the cottages she owned on the coast that were never locked anyway. Hughie didn't know what most of them opened, and he muttered about this as he searched for the right one.

"All these keys," he grumbled, "Just like her. Bottle tops. Jars. She had to collect the lot. Bet they're all in here too." Finally he found the key and it turned stiffly in the lock. He stood in the hall and breathed the musty, closed-in air of a house that has been shut up for a long time. He had expected to feel overwhelmed at once by a familiar odour, or the sense of home he dimly remembered from childhood, but this did not happen. He wasn't sure exactly how it should feel, but he felt there ought to be something, some recognition. In the driveway, Kate's old Studebaker sat on its belly in the dust. She used to come and visit in that car when they still lived out west — pot-plants along the back window, old blankets on the seats. She hung a faded towel in the front windscreen to act as a sunshield. Sheila used to complain: "Why can't she buy a regular cardboard one like everyone else? Safeway. Four dollars fifty. It wouldn't hurt."

Hughie blew dust off a photo of his parents that was on the hall stand. His mother's eyes squinted in the sun and there was the defiant uplift of the chin that was Kate's too. The photo frame left a gap in the dust and suddenly the whole place seemed to stare blearily at him from under a carpet of dust. Ten months of it clogged the house: he stopped in the door of the sitting room. He couldn't believe that such a short time could make the place look so bleak and uninhabited. The windows were thick with grime. Kate? She wasn't in this room. Not even her spirit was here. He touched the books on the shelves, ran a finger through the dust on the piano lid, but he did not touch any of the keys. The photos on the mantelpiece looked like anyone's family photographs: there he was, a fleshy scowling teenager, and Kate looking serious in spectacles, and Myron, the youngest, in the fork of a tree. He was there with Sheila and the kids — grouped awkwardly round the car on a family holiday, sunburned and grinning. Foolish, he looked, and he turned away ashamed.

Down in his studio on Redondo Beach, Marc Frostick was watching his girlfriend make a ballgown out of the duvet. She held it around her naked body and strutted in what she imagined was a sexy fashion across the room and back.

"D'you know what'd be *really* erotic?" Marc said in slow, exaggerated tones. The telephone rang and he leaned from the beanbag still grinning at her, to pick it up. "Hello, Marc Frostick?" His girlfriend wiggled her hips under the duvet. "Oh — hi dad!"

"IT'S MY DAD," he mouthed at her, with a kind of frenzied delight. She clapped both hands to her mouth to stifle a scream of laughter and the duvet dropped in a silent heap on the carpet.

"Well yeah, dad," he said soberly. "I'm kinda tied up all weekend here. Where ARE ya? Uh-huh, Kate's place. Right. Fresno." He covered the phone and mouthed, "HE'S WEIRD!" The girlfriend burst into fresh paroxysms of stifled laughter and sat down suddenly on the duvet.

"Well no, dad, I mean yeah, I got lots of schoolwork, y'know? I got summerschool finals in a week. Is mom there too? No? Tch. Look dad, I'd love to come up. It's just a bad time." He motioned to his girlfriend to put the duvet on again, and mouthed something indistinguishable. "Uh-huh. Yeah, I guess you will, dad... Did she? Yeah, I remember now. Aunt Kate was always collecting." The girl had the duvet round her neck now and was stalking slowly towards him, one bare leg showing. He put his hand over the mouthpiece — "She was WEIRD TOO!" — and the girl let out a little scream.

"Huh, I bet there is a lot of it... Well, like I said dad, any other time, y'know? Ok dad, yeah, I'm workin' hard alright... Ok... see yuh soon dad." He hung up, there was a moment of suspense, then the two of them indulged in a lengthy and painful bout of laughter which ended with them both on the floor, entangled in the duvet.

"No," gasped the boy, "D'you know what'd be REALLY SEXY though? A BALLGOWN WITH NOTHING UNDERNEATH IT!"

Hughie opened a jar of Kate's pickles at lunchtime. He'd brought food with him, bread, peanut butter, some tins of pork and beans. The onions were large and pellucid. Black peppers floated on the surface of the pickling fluid. Pickles keep forever, Hughie said to himself as he prised the jar open. Kate pickled everything, and what she couldn't pickle she cured or preserved or dried. There were shelves of food in her back larder — bottles and jars of stores she had laid by for winter, or guests... for what? Hughie wondered, gazing along the shelves. It was a pity to waste them, but there was a certain urgency to get the task underway and he began to search for plastic sacks. Halfway through the search, however, he came to a sort of stop. Hunched at the kitchen cabinet below the sink he left off searching for black sacks in the various places where Sheila always kept hers. It wasn't the search that seemed futile. It wasn't even the great task of clearing the house that had called for a week of his annual leave and the trip out west. Hughie was stopped in his tracks like a weighty animal, dimly aware that the light filtering down through the forest leaves was no longer enough. He was arrested by the notion that for some time now he had been blundering, muddling through. He struggled to put a name to the feeling. It had not only been with him since to coming to Kate's, the oddly disquieting conversation with his son, his ill-equipped battle with the house that had belonged to his dead sister and was now, until he could sell it, his. Abruptly he stood. It had settled on him, the futility of trying to see clearly. Furrowing his brow as though to recollect something, he walked uncertainly to the timber door that opened on the cellar steps. In the cellar there was more food and the accumulations of thirty years. Hughie scarcely glanced about him. On the front wall was Kate's wine cellar. The racks held twenty, maybe thirty bottles of wine — home brewed and vintage alike. Kate had loved a good wine. But Hughie reached out and took the first bottle that came to hand. Not pausing even to examine the label, he went heavily back up the cellar steps to the kitchen.

Sheila Frostick was worried and annoyed. In her annoyance she dialled a wrong number and called the Dunkin' Donuts on third street before she got through to her eldest daughter.

"Carole? Is that you?" she snapped. "Is your father there?" Her daughter was tired and she didn't know where her father was. The kids were home from school, a jaundice scare. She hadn't seen her father for some weeks.

"Well he's disappeared then," said her mother shortly. "He's not been home for two days. No note. Not a sign."

Carole thought she remembered something about a trip out west. To Aunt Kate's house. There was a brief silence.

"Ah. Well. That's that then. Have you had the children seen by a doctor?"

No, Carole hadn't been in touch with the doctor yet, it was just a scare.

"That's what you have to do then. You don't want them on your hands for weeks, do you?"

No, Carole didn't want that. Hadn't Hughie said anything about going away?

"That's your father all over," Sheila answered grimly. "He probably didn't even pack clean underwear."

Hughie *had* packed clean underwear. His small shabby suitcase sat on a high bed in Kate's back bedroom. In it were six pairs of shorts and six pairs of threadbare grey socks. Hughie himself, his senses dulled by half a bottle of excellent wine, was in the larder, filling sacks with the contents of the shelves. He worked methodically, and his mind did not stray very far from the task that employed him. At six o'clock, he stopped work and ate half a dozen picked onions, bread and cold beans, washed down with the rest of the wine. He slept a little in an armchair in the sitting room and when he woke it was getting dark. His head felt woolly and his movements were thick and clumsy. When he turned on the light nothing happened. Kate's electricity supply had long been disconnected, with his own permission, given from New York. Now he stood in the centre of the darkening room and the emptiness of his heart bore down on him. It threatened to crush him with a terrible weight he could not understand or describe to himself. He gave a low groan. The streetlights flickered on, casting pale silver squares in the room, on the walls and on the bare boards. It was really quite a beautiful light. He turned to the black space of the doorway. He said his sister's name once, questioningly, but she did not appear. He lay down on the old stuffed sofa with the patchwork rug and pulled this about him, gripping his own body with his arms as though in the night he might freeze to death. He did not remove his shoes.

The Test

Sara Berkeley

No motion has she now, no force;
She neither hears nor sees;
Rolled round in earth's diurnal course,
With rocks, and stones, and trees.

6pm Tuesday

I wouldn't have started in this colour of fear, but every evening around now — five, six, seven — it gets dark like this. Big storm clouds mass up and yesterday a bolt of lightning forked down like a snake's tongue and bit into the scaffolding outside. I ran into the hallway and put on a pair of rubber-soled shoes and felt how my heart was banging.

"My heart is really banging!" I said aloud, experimentally, and it was a little calming to hear the words in my own voice. At the same time the skin under prickled unpleasantly and I felt hot and weak.

I got courage washing, climbing those wooden steps to the laundry room. Only a couple of weeks ago the heat up there was red, but last night we were cold. The sun went down astonishingly, angrily. We began to feel the awful quiet dark, gathering in the flat.

"Let's go to Lola's party," I said, not believing we would.

"Alright. Let's." Al said, and we both got our coats at once, because to hesitate would mean sitting in the dark until it was time to go to bed.

The party was a strange animal; my old friends didn't seem to want to know me any more, and I didn't want to go in where there was dancing, and it was cold. In bed later, my feet would not warm up. Al slept, his arm flung across the sheet. He was frightened.

At two in the morning, a man was shouting drunk in the car park. All down the street he flickered in and out of peoples' dreams. Sleep pawed blindly at my window and into the room the man stumbled, holding a green glass bottle and shouting out the test results. "Oh no," I mumbled, coming half awake at the same time, "it's my fault..." On and on he was shouting, a litany of medical terms. I couldn't quite hear them but I knew what they were and I twisted in the bed to make him stop. Even then, when I was fully awake, and the strips of light were as they were every night on the bedroom wall, I felt I knew without question what the man had been shouting.

I dragged myself up in the bed until I could see over the windowsill. It took me awhile to make him out, sitting on a curb with his legs spread out in front of him and a white singlet on. Was he only wearing a singlet in the night? I felt suddenly sick with shame, lying there watching him, hiding below the window ledge. I slid back down in the bed. The quilt was too heavy now. "Don't leave!" the man shouted. They were too clear, the words. I watched the clock until it was nearly three.

This morning we sat in the sitting-room and could not leave. There are days like that: they will not begin. Some band was singing on the radio, 'I don't know why sometimes I get frigh-tened'. Al was terribly quiet. Then a Beatles song. They play three or four in an hour, the oldest songs, full of Sunday mornings when I was a kid. What's wrong with remembering? On Christmas morning we had to wait for the grandmothers to come back from church in fur coats. Then we could open the presents.

"Come on," Al said in the end. "Let's go."

Walking round the lake, the sunshine was stiff and the clouds very high up and innocent. By five they would be like this, towering and jealous.

At the station we saw a blind man who was lost. He was banging into things with his stick and shouting, "I'm blind and I need some help." At first, we held back, wanting to avoid it, the naked white stick. Blind people always seem so capable. They tap the wall, they stop at curbs, they pause to get their bearings, then go on. No-one ever shouted for help like this before. Then we both felt ashamed at the same time and started forward. The man clung to my arm, while we led him down to the trains. He said hardly anything, but held on and I thought, "I'll be able to feel his hand gripping my arm long after he has gone." He talked a little but he seemed gruff and I was impatient and ashamed and sorry. I could hardly make my brain think about being blind. It was more like repeating in fear, "I don't want to be blind! I don't want to be blind!" and without transition I was telling myself I did not want to die.

1pm Wednesday

I found I had written words without even hearing what the lecturer said. I was high up in one of the larger theatres. The gradient was vertiginous. I crept in late and sat shaking at the back, trying to slip into the atmosphere of the class, the casual attention, feet on the chairbacks, occasional notes. The dream of last night blossomed in my head and I sat very still, trying to recapture the emotional atmosphere that coloured the dream, that seemed strangely separate from what went on. I was up at night looking after my grandfather and we both knew, sort of amusedly, that he was going to die. When the time came, he stood up and he was in my arms at a shelf or desk, and then *I* was in someone's arms and I was doing the dying and I hoped it would be over quickly without any great pain at the heart. I was ready, and then it came and it was over and I was just sort of calm. I laid him out and left the room to wake my parents and tell them it was done.

Dante, I had written Halfway through my life I woke up in a dark forest. Virgil guides him through the Inferno and Purgatory, and Beatrice brings him to Paradise. Virgil his favourite poet. Beatrice his love. Who will guide me through the Inferno? Gertrude Stein wrote a poem that went something like: "Yes yes yes yes yes yes you bet yes certainly yes yes no." The Frosts had five children but lost one. *No motion has she now, no force; She neither hears nor sees...*

I was writing the words as I heard them, in a kind of panic. It was so lonely sitting there, all of life just coming and going, coming and going, sleeping and waking.

"That's what poetry is — it's a twin flower — tries to say both things at the same time."

I looked up from my frantic scribbling. People were sitting with their eyes closed. There were the usual huddles of two, whispering, a hand on a girl's back, moving up and down the cotton. I got up in a hurry and left. It was over anyway. Two hours to go now. Halfway through my life I woke up in a dark forest.

2pm Wednesday

I ate no lunch again. For the second day I queued in two different sandwich bars and watched with growing nausea as people ordered sandwiches and picked apples or chocolate bars. Just short of the counter I felt light-headed, the pounding started and I turned away. I sat on the grass between attempts to buy some lunch, until there was no point any longer. There were disconnected phrases from the lecture in my head, and names that hung together in bunches, the late Victorians, the Modernists, the pre-Raphaelites. "What shall we do," I murmured and got up to walk. Three o'clock, they said. It is scarcely two. The hospital is at the north end of the campus. You cling on to your health hungrily in a hospital and you want to be seen to be carrying the flowers. The place smells of fear: there is such a smell. Dogs catch it, and rabbits give it off. I would try to write to my mother but it would make me cry and I would have to give up. You know that feeling after you've cried a lot: like a beach after heavy waves. Flotsam and jetsam. Al and I in the water on a Greek beach last summer: "I'm Flotsam." "Hi Flotsam! I'm Jetsam."

2.30pm Wednesday

I passed the cool green slope where I often lie reading, watching a football game, with the sounds of water from the swimming pool. It would be nice to lie face down in the grass, but I cannot sleep or lie down. I am vertical, like Sylvia Plath. I thought of her with her two kids in a flat on Primrose Hill. I don't know if I was more scared on my own, when it was just me who knew, or after I told Al. He got terribly quiet and still. Then it was a reality, I have not written it down. Some time the point comes where childhood must stop and you can never look back in the same way as you did. You wish for it to be the same as it was; it was warm and comfortable, it was dull, and even that seems enviable. It can never be the same. Look forward. Carry out the simple tasks — put the washing in the dryer and keep vertical.

Nothing is quite normal. O God, *purifiez nos coeurs*. I'm going now.

Friday the first

A new month and I hope we always remember Wednesday as the day the scare lifted oh I hope we never forget that date for that and what a scare I wouldn't have had it happen that way but the tests showed negative and Al was laughing on the phone when I said it's all alright Al and we came quickly out of the fright and we are out the other side and in clear air and sunshine and we shiver and laugh with relief and I know this is a hopelessly long sentence but that is just what life is going to be from now on just a long sentence with no punctuation until a full stop at the end.

Saxifrage

Sara Berkeley

The woman was talking about kids on drug programmes and Marcia blinked several times as though clearing her vision would help her remember her name. She looked away briefly. Maybe looking freshly at the woman would bring the name back. Across the room Frank was in an attitude of leaving. He stood uncertainly talking to Sam Moreau's wife and he was trying to wrap up the conversation. He put his empty glass on the bookshelf behind him and nodded quickly several times. Marcia realised with a constriction around her heart that he was going to come over to her and they would leave then. They were going away from this room where people stood at the french doors eating pineapple and cheese on cocktail sticks and sat on the couches with their shoes kicked off talking animatedly about houseplants and shares.

She hadn't wanted to come. A lot of people gathering at the Harris's on a Sunday afternoon, talking about the same old things. She had left it until the last moment to dress. While Frank put on a shirt and tie she sat in the old red armchair looking at a magazine, her legs tucked under her. She wasn't even wearing stockings. Then Frank was in the hall, fixing his tie at the mirror, and she flicked the pages faster, seeing only a blur of car advertisements — he was in the doorway looking down at her and she knew his expression without meeting his eye.

"Shall we hit the road then?" Frank passed his hand down her back now, and smiled at the woman. "Hi Bonnie."

"Oh," Marcia felt a sudden need to hear Bonnie talk on about the kids on drug programmes. "Frank—" she felt a little short of breath, "Bonnie was just telling me something very interesting, weren't you Bonnie?" She turned back to the woman and smiled uncertainly. It was a pleasure to say the name and she wanted the opportunity to use it a few more times, to talk on about the kids and other things, to ask Bonnie what she did, where she worked, if she had kids herself.

"We'd better go," Frank said decisively. Marcia felt defeated. They had to leave. Some couples had already gone, there was a knot of people in the hall promising they would call one another. Bonnie was ready to turn to someone else.

"Don't you think," Marcia burst out as though with the last of her breath, "it's odd to be leaving a party just after six? Afternoon parties are so... strange!" She *was* feeling strange. Twenty past six, they were leaving a party. Sunday. What was she normally doing at twenty past six on a Sunday? Frank held her arm and was leading her to the door. She took a last look over her shoulder. Bonnie had her bag open and was rummaging as though for a lipstick. "Bye Bonnie!" she called brightly. Bonnie looked up briefly but didn't seem to see her.

Frank steered her firmly down the hall. She knew several of the people vaguely but there was no time to do more than call goodbye. Lynn Harris was standing at the top of the stairs with two men. Frank called to her that it had been a lovely afternoon and she waved a cigarette lighter at them. Call us back, Marcia thought. Tell us we mustn't go yet. But Lynn was telling a funny story to her guests. Marcia looked at the flowers bordering their front path. The lawn was freshly mowed and the smell of damp cut grass brought a pang to her heart. Her father, cutting the lawn on a Saturday, his hair flopping down in his eyes and his unlit pipe clenched grimly between his teeth. What were those small pink flowers? You could chew the stems, they had a bitter flavour. She used to do it as a kid. Not alyssum, that was white. These were little pink, fragile things.

"Marcia," Frank said. She was standing on the other side of the car from him, staring across the roof. "I've opened it." The car was blue. Was it theirs? Surely their car wasn't blue. She bent down and peered in at the back window. That was how you knew your own car when you came out of the shopping centre or the airport: the old maps, wrappers, gloves. There was a Mars wrapper and a yellowed newspaper. Could be anyone's car. But Frank was starting up and leaning over and tapped on her window. "It's open!" she heard him repeat, through the glass. His voice was faraway. If she stayed out here, on the curb, would he drive away without her? Sitting into the passenger seat she saw herself going back up the path and into the clogged hall. She could find Bonnie and ask about the drug programme. She could ask her if she knew what the pink flowers were called.

They turned out onto the main road from the Harris's quiet street. "Bob's been playing golf all week," Frank said. "Says his swing's got ten times better. He's looking great, actually." He checked his mirror and changed lanes. "He's in deep mourning for Greta Garbo. Got six of her films out on video on Tuesday." Greta Garbo, Marcia thought, Marilyn Monroe, Brigitte Bardot. Seems like it helped to have your name end in 'o' if you wanted to be a film star. Frank was heading for the freeway exit and she realised uneasily they'd soon be on the bridge. The sky was gathering a sort of deep grey. It looked huge, a tremendous expanse across the bay, with the moving pinpricks of planes. More cars coming back down to the valley than heading east across the bridge. Couldn't they go back? You didn't turn on the freeway, it had to be now, on the main road. Couldn't they turn and go the way everyone else was going? Back to the party. Mombresia, was that the name? No, they'd been in the garden too, along the wall, tightly closed. Mombresia were orange and flowered in July. She smoothed her skirt down and watched the cars as they reached the entrance to the freeway. So fast! And all going somewhere. They all knew where they were going.

"You look lovely in that," Frank said suddenly. She was surprised, and glanced at him.

"This," she said anxiously. He'd had a haircut that Friday and the cropped hairs at the base of his neck seemed to bristle. She was afraid of the look, it was a severe haircut, ugly. His hand on the gearstick seemed perilously close to her leg, almost touching but not quite. They might touch any moment if the car went over a bump.

San Mateo Bridge 3. The sign went over their heads. Three miles left and then the long arm out into the bay, skinny and crooked like an old man's.

"Rita's going to quit her job," Frank said. "She reckons she'll never move up in there. She's got ambition."

Marcia closed her eyes. They were burning, as though she'd been crying. Staring into the dusk did it. Never read when the light's going, her father always said, you don't realise how dark it is, the change is gradual. She opened them again and it seemed a lot darker. The last light was behind them, wasn't it? So they were heading into the dark, plunging right into night. All those cars were following the last of the light. Why were they running from it?

The car climbed the ramp onto the bridge and the steel girders loomed over them. Grey bars on both sides. And below — the water! Frank had begun to hum. They were streaming in a flow of cars along a narrow road needling precariously into the Bay. It was so fragile. Couldn't they stay on land? She felt her stomach contract. It was dreadful, this intrusion out over the water. It was a thing of man. Nature meant people to stay on the land. Small boats rocking, tiny specks in the mass of water, capsized. Huge ocean liners were crushed by icebergs and went down, sucking the air into a huge trough after them, disappearing, without a trace.

"Frank," she said loudly. It was necessary they go back at once. They were already in sight of the slope down the causeway part; the knotty old man's elbow, the rheumy joint. It was too late!

"I don't want to be on the bridge," she said, but she seemed to speak in a tiny voice, hardly audible over the rushing in her ears, certainly not over the noise of the engine. They were doing seventy.

"You don't want to what?" Frank said. He was changing into the fast lane. She shook her head. The little pink flowers — why couldn't she remember the name? It began with S. Not sassafras, not sassafras, that was a tree.

She gripped her hands tightly together and the car took the bend of the bridge smoothly. The causeway! Now they were on the narrow stretch running straight across to the East Bay. Seven miles, she remembered it was that far across to the shore. Surely it couldn't be that far? The lights on the other side were well defined now, winking in the hills and in lines along the roads. People were going home. What were they going home from at seven on a Sunday evening? The game? Too late for church. Little back streets where the dark was swallowing up houses. Bad lighting. It was swallowing up whole roads, blanketing the things that went on there, things that were only done in the secrecy of darkness. If it could just hold off for a bit! Her mind paused on the brink of a dark street in the city and edged down close to a high wall. Graffiti, broken glass. The further in, the darker it would get, and all the secrets that the dark kept, she found herself holding her breath tightly — it was fearful things, murders, stabbings, rape, they were all going on, at that moment, over there in the stretch of bulky land they were racing towards. She shook her head quickly as though to rid her mind of the images but they were gathering there, broken windows, shadowy figures, hands raised in violence. She felt dread grip her. They must turn back! How many miles left? Six? Five?

"Frank," she said again, feeling panic tighten her throat. "Let's go back."

He heard her but she hoped he didn't detect the panic. She mustn't appear irrational. Was it irrational not ever to want to reach the shore? Wasn't the bridge as bad, that narrow sliver of earth?

"Huh? Back?"

"No, no," she retracted hurriedly. To reach the shore would be to get off the bridge. But the darkness! The crimes that would be springing up everywhere, doors beaten down, bottles smashing, children would be screaming; it was children who suffered, and young girls. Frank had said something. She took a deep breath.

"No, not back. How far is it to shore now?"

"Well I dunno. About four miles. Looks pretty, doesn't it?"

Pretty? Even the lights were menacing. Tiny wicked pin-pricks, sharp stars. What were the flowers called? Abruptly she began to cry, convulsive sobs, the tears running unchecked down her cheeks and dripping onto the silk blouse Frank thought she looked lovely in. All the way to the shore she cried, with Frank offering to pull over, to stop the car, asking her over and over what the matter was. What was the matter? She held her temples and kept her eyes tightly shut, the land getting closer and closer. What was the *matter*?

Frank checked his mirror and brought the car to the side of the road where there was a stretch of gravel. They were off the bridge, off the freeway, back on the road to their hometown. It was a deserted district, old warehouses, silent trucks. He reached across and laid a hand on his wife's knee.

"Marcia, what is it? Tell me."

"I can't—" she began tearfully, "I can't remember the name of those little pink flowers. You know the ones—" she gave a sob — "the ones Lynn has by her path. They're pink." She hid her face in her hands and sobbed. "You can eat the stems."

The Clouds In My Eyes

James LaBudde

I take Danny out to my car. His hand is clutched at my elbow and his long white cane, tucked under his arm, points behind him like an animal's raised tail. The car is parked off the curb and I tell him, "Down a step."

He sits in the passenger seat and I load his suitcase into the trunk. I see his name on the luggage tag, printed in the tight scrawl of my mother's hand. There is a second set of tags, these are imprinted with the raised dots of Braille. I touch it, my fingers are thick and rough and the Braille is impossibly small. How does he do it? How does my little brother, little Danny, do it? I jerk my hand away feeling guilty and ashamed.

I get into the car and we pull out to the street. Danny is pressed against his door, the window is down, and his face is stuck into the wind like a Labrador retriever's.

"Looks like it might rain," I say.

"Smells like it."

I steer up onto the highway on-ramp, gun the engine, and settle into a solid fifty-five mph. The airport is about twenty miles away. I look at the digital clock and calculate our driving time. Danny will make his plane with an hour to spare.

As we drive, there is a growing silence that hangs between us like some invisible mass. I decide I must say something before it's too late. Before Danny assumes I don't want to talk and I don't want him to talk.

"We've discussed the weather," I say. "Now what?"

"How about the obvious?"

I look over at him as he cranks the window up and straightens back in the seat. He is bracing himself. Then he says; "Now's your chance. Give it to me."

I adjust the rearview mirror. I pull at my seat belt. I tap my fingers on the wheel.

He can't wait for me any longer.

"I know exactly what you want to say," he says.

"Am I that transparent?"

"Saran Wrap."

"Tell me then. I want to hear it from you."

"Okay." He rubs his palms back and forth across his thighs. "You're going to start out by telling me how you're sure I can take care of myself, how amazed you are at the things I can do — that a blind person can do. You're gonna say, you've never doubted me, never underestimated me, and that you've never felt sorry for me."

"That's good. Keep going."

"You'll segue into a litany of 'buts'. Like... But how will you get around? But what will you do if you get lost? But what if someone takes advantage of you or robs you?"

"And all good buts, you must admit?"

"None that I haven't already thought about."

"Except... you left out one."

"Yeah?"

"But why, Danny? Why do you have to do it? You're blind for chrissake — blind people don't travel to Europe. It makes no sense."

He shakes his head.

"Why, Danny, goddammit?"

"Daniel. Please call me, Daniel."

"You're never gonna be Daniel to me, okay? You got Mom and Dad to call you that, all our relatives, but don't think I'm gonna do it. I don't care if it makes you sound like a kid. You act like a kid, don't you? You're acting like a kid now, this whole Europe thing is something a kid would do."

My fingers are going a mile a minute — tapping, tugging, picking. Danny is rubbing his palms again. We both share the family trait of nervous hands.

Then Danny changes the subject.

"Remember the time we climbed the train trestle?"

"What? Yeah, the one that went over Route 38."

"We climbed up the wooden frame, getting splinters as thick as match sticks stuck into our hands. You had the cans of spray paint tucked into your belt and every time you bent at the waist they would squirt a circle of orange paint onto your shirt.

"And when we finally got to the top, bloody, sweaty, covered in paint, we stood on the train tracks and screamed, Top of the world, Ma! Top of the world! like we were a couple of maniacs. Like we were James Cagney.

"Then an eighteen-wheel semi came barreling down Route 38 and the driver sees us standing up on the trestle and like a jerk he blows his air horn."

"It scared the shit out me!" I say.

"Yeah, me too. I thought a train was coming. I almost jumped over the side I was so scared. But then we hung out over the side of the trestle and spray painted our names for all the passing cars to see. For the whole world to see."

"And you were so stupid you painted your first and last name! Big block letters you wrote, Danny Newman! I still can't believe you did that."

"It made us famous didn't it? Everybody knew who the Newman boys were after that."

"Including the police! I'm still amazed we didn't get arrested."

We don't talk for a couple minutes. Both of us remembering what it was like to be kids. To be brothers.

"Hey!" Danny screams.

"What?"

"The Water Gun Shoot-out at the A&P Corral!"

"God... Remember how pissed mom was? I can still hear her screaming at me."

"Well, you were supposed to be selling papers. I used to watch you after school standing in front of the A&P yelling, Paaaaper, Paaaaper, Evenin' Indepeeeendent. It was like a song, the way you did that."

"It sold papers."

"And then me and Scotty Pendergrass attacked you with our new machine gun squirt guns. We soaked you. And most of your papers."

"But I got you back. I ran into the Rexall Drug Store, and used all my paper money to buy the biggest squirt gun they had."

"Yeah, it was just too bad that mom drove up to do some grocery shopping, just as you were chasing me through the parking lot."

"She grabbed me by the ear and dragged me back to the front of the A&P, screaming, This is not a playground, young man, this is your job! This is where you work! Then she saw the stack of wet newspapers, and grabbed the squirt gun out of my hand and stomped on it. Little pieces of plastic went flying everywhere. Out into the parking lot, across the sidewalk, into the A&P. I bet there's still bits of that gun laying around there."

"But she never punished me." Danny says.

"Of course not. You weren't supposed to be working. You were a kid, a baby. And if I recall, you and Scotty Pendergrass went into the drugstore and had french fries and cherry cokes. While I sold soggy newspapers until nine o'clock that night."

The exit for the airport comes and I follow the signs for departing passengers. I stop the car in front of the terminal and turn off the engine. I figure I have to try one last time.

"Danny, please don't go. You don't have to go, you can stay here and we can do some more things together."

"Not anymore, bro. I ain't the same, you're not the same. Nothing is since I went blind."

"No, Danny. We can be. We can try. This Europe thing, I don't understand it, it's stupid. You don't need to go, you don't need to take that kind of chance."

"I want to."

"That's not a good enough reason. I'm sorry, that doesn't cut it with me."

"Okay," he says. "I'll try to explain it to you, I don't know if I can, but I'll try."

"All right."

"When I started going blind, I was only seventeen years old. Seventeen. You were twenty, and going to college, living away from home, working part-time at the school book store. And when you came home to visit me, to visit your blind little brother, you were different."

"No. I was the same, Danny. I never treated you any different."

"I'm not saying you treated me different. I'm saying 'you' were different. You'd grown-up. You were an adult. Only there I was, not just struggling with the blindness, but also struggling with what you'd already done. You got to get out and become a person. You got the chance to prove to mom and dad that you were somebody. But me... I had to have mom cut my goddamm steak! I had dad driving me around like a fucking cab driver! I couldn't go outside alone, I couldn't play sports or games... It took me months to figure out how to go to the toilet by myself!

"But you did all that, Danny. You managed, you fought it, you struggled and learned. Look at you, you did it! You never gave up."

"Don't you see, bro? I was tossed back into the nest. Because of the blindness I never got to face the world and face real life. Succeed or fail, stand or fall, it doesn't matter what would've happened to me. But hell, I never got the chance! Yeah, sure everyone was so proud of me, you were proud of me for coming through like a trooper. I finished school, I even got a job. But nobody treated me like an adult. I was always the hopeless blind kid! Even to you, you still say what a kid I am. How I'm always, Little Danny! But dammit, I was never given the chance to show what I could do, what I could be!

"I never got the chance to become Daniel."

He opens the car door, takes his cane from the back seat, walks around the car and waits for me to pop the trunk. Then he takes out his suitcase with the two sets of luggage tags and he walks into the terminal.

I jump out of the car, running behind him, tripping over suitcases and bumping into the Skycaps. I see him talking to someone, and then he turns toward the check-in line.

I follow him. I'm nervously rubbing my fingers together. Things are getting cloudy, my eyes are stinging.

He hears my footsteps and turns to me and opens his arms. He hugs me, and I try to speak, but for some reason I can't. He says;

"Good-bye, bro. I'll send you a postcard from Gibraltar."

And I squeeze him as tight as I can, and finally manage to say, "Good-bye, Daniel."

Daniel is traveling tonight on a plane.
I can see the red tail-lights, heading for Spain.
And I can see Daniel waving good-bye.
God, it looks like Daniel,
Must be the clouds in my eyes.

Postcard From Big Sky

James LaBudde

Stretched across the back seat of Mother's Dodge Dart, feet stuck out the window, hot summer air and crunchy flying insects careening against my toes. Mother drives and sings along to the song, 'Kung Fu Fighting', which is battling the static on the AM radio and the static is winning. Looking straight up and out the other window into a blue sky.

Occasionally, a pathetic little cloud in the shape of a small tit will float by. Eyes closed and feel a stinging burn, open the eyes and wait for a better class of cloud.

"Welcome to Wyoming!" Mother says.

"The Cowboy State, or, The Equality State."

"That's right, honey. You haven't missed one since Iowa."

"That's okay, Mother. No one even knows what a Hawkeye is." And Iowa clouds are shit.

Mother begins to sing along to the song, 'American Pie'. She thinks she knows the words, but really only remembers the part about driving the Chevy to the levee but the levee was dry.

It was Mother's idea to take this trip. Not that I argued. I'd spent enough summers at our City Recreation Center (or as it's more commonly known to its members, The Titty Masturbation Center). The Rec Center is basically a field of dirt and a bunker-shaped gymnasium that smells like vomit. You are lucky to find a basketball that isn't flat, a ping-pong ball that hasn't been crushed, or a badminton racket that isn't cracked. And the only kids that ever go there are fat and asthmatic, or skinny and allergic to everything, or small-for-their-age guys who would really rather read a book than play kickball — only their mothers have to work all day and don't like the idea of their baby being home all alone with his head in a book when it's such a nice sunny day outside. But you see, Mother, nice days don't mean shit to me. I've always preferred cloudy days. You can lay on the sofa and read a good book and no-one will bother you about it. And if there are no good books left you can always look at the big, dark, awesome clouds.

Sweat glues me to the seat. Roll onto my side and look under the front seat, there are my sneakers and dirty socks, a twice-read paperback book, an empty A&W root beer can, and three crusty pennies. Grab the book, 'Slaughterhouse Five', by Kurt Vonnegut, scan for the good parts.

Eyes begin to sting, drop the book, check for clouds.

"Welcome to Montana!" Mother says.

"The Treasure State, or the Big Sky State."

"You are good, you know that? All that reading, I guess."

Sitting up in the seat.

"Hey! The Big Sky State, Mother!"

"Yes, I heard you."

Head jerks around, eyes scan the horizon. North, south, east, west, nothing but blue.

"And not a single cloud!"

"Nope."

"No clouds!"

"It's just not the right time of year, I guess, baby."

Fall back with a heavy sigh.

"Not even in Montana."

"What's that?"

"I mean, shit, what's the use of having all that extra sky if they're not going to do anything with it?"

"It does look bigger, doesn't it? Maybe you could look in one of your books and find out why?"

Stretch out, put the feet in the window, look up into the burning blue.

"I already know why. No clouds. It's The Big Sky, No Cloud State!"

Mother ignores me and begins to sing, 'Suspicious Minds', she thinks she knows the words, but really only knows the part about caught in a trap, and I can't walk out.

Kick the car door.

"Shit State!"

"Enough, already! It's just sky, for chrissake!"

"No, Mother. It's Big Sky, and getting bigger all the time."

Sex, Love, and Baseball — After the Apocalypse

James LaBudde

How it all started

I was in my local bar, the Sunset Inn, playing a game of eight-ball and drinking Pabst Blue Ribbon beer. There was talcum powder on my hands and specks of blue chalk under my fingernails. Behind the bar a TV set was blaring the game show 'Jeopardy' and Alex Trebeck was chiding a contestant for not phrasing their answer in the form of a question.

Suddenly, Alex was gone and in his place was Peter Jennings of ABC News. Peter Jennings said that China had invaded the Soviet Union and the United States would be joining forces with the Soviets. He also said that the President feared nuclear activity was imminent.

There were only three other people in the bar. None of them seemed in the least bit worried. "Let them fight it out over there," said Small Bones Baker from his bar stool. "What do we care if the Ruskies and the Chinks kill themselves off?"

But I was worried. I set my pool cue down on the table and walked out. This was the day I was waiting for. The day I dreaded, yet always knew deep down would come.

I got into my truck and drove straight home. No stops, no last minute shopping at the 7-Eleven. You're not supposed to have to think as the world burns down.

I pulled into my driveway and jumped out of the truck. I walked into the house and straight into the bomb shelter. So what if the lights and the gas were still on? So what. The end of the world was coming.

Why I survived

In 1955 my father decided to build either a bomb shelter or a greenhouse, both of which he could order plans for from 'Popular Mechanics' magazine. He finally chose the bomb shelter, which at the time wasn't so unusual. The country was in the middle of the Cold War and everyone thought the Russians were going to drop an atom bomb on us at any moment. I remember going to school and seeing films about it. For months I had visions of mushroom clouds as I lay in bed trying to sleep.

So Dad began going down into the basement everyday after work and staying there until ten or eleven at night. He would haul down bricks and cement and we'd hear loud banging and the sad whine of power tools while watching TV. Sometimes I would go down and sit on a bucket and watch him. He seemed very concerned about filling all the little cracks.

When the bomb shelter was finished my father stocked it with canned goods and bottled water and hung up an American flag. Then as quickly as he became obsessed with it — he lost interest. The bomb shelter went the the way of the home beer-making kit and the chinchilla cages. We eventually ended up using it to store Christmas ornaments and paint cans.

But I didn't forget about the shelter. And after a bad day at school or a fight with my parents, I would go down there to be by myself. I felt secure, with my back up against the cold concrete and the strong smell of paint and turpentine making me lightheaded. I used to imagine that I was a five star general and the country was at war with the Nazis. The Nazis made much better enemies than the Russians.

The Sixties came and I went off to Vietnam. After failing almost every entry test I landed a job working in Military Intelligence. I still wonder how I ever got out of that place alive. That's also when I came to realize that our country was being run by a bunch of assholes and few of the people in power could be trusted.

When I left 'Nam I went to work in Alaska. I thought I would be safe up there near the top of the world, and one summer I talked my parents into flying up for a vacation. I told them all about the hunting and fishing and the month-long days. I didn't tell them that their plane might crash over the Yukon. But it did.

At the funeral, and for days after, I kept waiting for the tears to come. But I was tougher than I thought. Then I moved back into my parents' old house and I went down to Dad's bomb shelter. It was cool and dark and it still smelled exactly the same. I pressed my back up against that cold cement wall just like I did as a boy.

I think I cried a little.

But the house held too many memories within the old plaid furniture and the lime green kitchen cabinets. So to make it livable I gutted it and redecorated. The only thing I didn't change was the bomb shelter.

What I heard

I was in the bomb shelter two days when I felt a small jolt and heard a low rumbling like far off thunder. The bombs had come. It was the first day of the rest of all life. I laughed out loud.

What I did

The first few weeks passed easily enough. To keep busy I did a lot of reading and painting. I painted murals on the walls and when I ran out of space I just painted over the old ones.

I spent a lot of time thinking about a woman — the last woman I saw before I went down to the shelter. She was sitting in the Sunset Inn and drinking Lambrusco. I remember she was very tan and her bra strap was sticking out the side of her tank top. If I closed my eyes I didn't see her face, all I saw was that white bra strap against her tan shoulder.

I didn't know the woman's name. So I began to call her Tina because she looked like a Tina. It's funny how you can miss someone you never knew. I guess I was lonely.

I decided the first thing I would do when I got out was to go look for Tina. Or her dead body.

My dreams

I kept having the same dream:

I'm at a baseball game. It's the Phillies and the Mets and I'm sitting up in the stands behind right field. Suddenly, air raid sirens go off. But no-one else hears them. I try to warn everyone. I scream, "Can't you hear! The bombs are coming! The bombs are coming!" But they laugh, and won't listen. As I'm leaving the stadium Howard Johnson comes to the plate. He hits a fast ball that soars over the back fence. It hits me on the head and I fall to the ground. When I finally regain consciousness, the bombs have dropped and my skin has burned black. I wake up all hot and sweaty.

Food

I ate more food than I was supposed to, more than the allotted daily rations. Probably because I was bored. The food supply began to get very low.

Some of the foods I missed were: fresh corn on the cob, shrimp cocktail, butter pecan ice cream, french fries, Shakey's pizza, tangerines, watermelon, biscuits and gravy.

Some of the food I got sick of: anything in a can.

Sex

Me and the magazines.

After six months

The paint ran out.

The supply of books didn't last. I read through all of the John D. MacDonalds, all of the Tom Clancys, and even all the filler stories that were sandwiched between the nude pictures of mammoth-breasted woman in the 'Playboy' magazines. All that was left was the Bible.

I got really low on food.

I drew a set of lips and eyes on my hands and did Señor Wences imitations for hours.

I read the Bible.

The decision

I decided to leave the shelter. I didn't care about the radiation, the nuclear winter or the dog-sized rats. I was bored and lonely, and feared losing my sanity.

Outside

I opened the steel door on the shelter and there was rubble all around. The house had burned down and black timbers and ashes lay everywhere. But the sun was shining and the birds were singing.

My truck looked fine, still parked in the driveway where I had left it.

The rest of the neighborhood was still standing! All the other houses in perfect condition. I was in shock. I figured that it must have been a direct hit on my house.

Then I saw one of my neighbors watering his lawn. He was very surprised to see me. He said:

"I thought you died when your house blew up."

"My house blew up?" I said.

"Well, yeah... lightning struck it during that big thunderstorm."

I didn't know what to do. So I got in my truck and drove to the Sunset Inn. I sat there all day drinking beer and eating french fries.

Then Tina walked in.

My heart began to thump in my chest. I'd been waiting for this moment since the Apocalypse.

I went right up to her and started talking.

We sat and talked all night. She was still very tan and she said I looked pale. Turns out her real name is Kelly — but she said I could call her Tina. She gave me a goodbye kiss with wine-flavored lips.

The future

Tina/Kelly and I have a date this Friday night.

Baseball

The New York Mets won the pennant on a home run by Howard Johnson. Just like in my dream. Life is weird.

Going Under

Piers Letcher

There was a certain giddiness, freshness, about driving out of London at 6am on a June morning, the sky pale blue above her, the light sharp and hard and bright along the pavements. The city was asleep still, though the dawn providers of the essentials were out in force — newspaper boys, milkmen, postmen, small vans unloading outside corner shops. The first traffic was coming in from the outer suburbs, avoiding the rush hour, and she was steering the big BMW away, away from James, away from that snoring figure with the quilt wrapped around him like some giant pupa about to metamorphose. But Fiona had given up hope of James ever metamorphosing — he would just get richer, more successful, more establishment every year.

She reached for a tape and plugged it in, and the car was suddenly filled with a Mozart mass. So this was what James listened to on the way to work. She felt half-disappointed it wasn't one of those maddeningly popular soft rock bands; what did they call it? AOR? How was it that she didn't know he liked Mozart after fourteen years of marriage? Judging by the volume he loved Mozart. Yet they'd never heard Mozart at home. When people came round it was Dire Straits and Phil Collins and Sting.

You can live with someone for years, know things about them that no-one else could possibly know — the arm reaching vaguely for the off switch on the alarm; the glance at the just-used toilet paper — things that nobody would even want to know. And then you suddenly discover something fundamental about them and realise that maybe you were the only one who didn't know. Half of south-east London knew about James's affair with Mozart.

She looked down at her handbag, and absently stroked the silk scarf tied through the calfskin handle. The bag had been a present to herself in Italy, the scarf a Paris indulgence. The kind of things she would like James to give her — but James only ever bought her jewellery or trinkets for mantelpieces.

She swerved to avoid a newspaper boy on a tough-looking mountain bike and he swore viciously at her and gave her the finger, American style. He probably wasn't more than fourteen or fifteen and she felt out of her depth driving this expensive car. It wasn't the first time, but it was the first time without James there giving an uninterrupted flow of directions: You can overtake here — change down a gear — you need third on this bend — mind the man behind you — you can pull out now — after the third car, the red one.

She fiddled with the pearls in her necklace.

The tape finished as she drove through the outer suburbs. She watched the motorway sign approaching, vaguely registered the 'Dover' sign as it flashed past, an expanding blur of white on blue, and put her foot down. The car surged forward. It wasn't like driving her Escort at all.

She reached down for a new tape and came up with another surprise. Beethoven. It was one of the symphonies — she hadn't heard it since she'd been at school. The Third? The Seventh? She remembered hearing it in the cathedral when she was selling programmes for the school. All those coins. It all seemed so long ago. It was definitely the Seventh.

She was driving fast now — over a hundred she realised — and she drifted quietly past the trucks in the inside lane. She slowed as she spotted a police car on one of the motorway bridges.

Her music teacher had tried to explain Beethoven. He'd given each girl in the class — there were only half a dozen — a pair of ear-plugs to wear, and then made them play the piano. The notes sounded flat and dull and distant, and made her eyes water. Then he'd played while she held her head against the waxed side of the piano. She remembered the quick shiver that ran down her spine as she felt the music resonate inside her. The sensation of warm polished wood on her cheek and the faint smell of resin in the music room. She thought of the poor man writing his most famous works in a cold upstairs room, totally deaf, smashing pianos to destruction in frustration and despair.

She was already approaching Dover. It was extraordinary — she felt like she'd only just left home. She drove down to the Eastern docks, and found a parking place in a small street with the houses tucked right under the cliff. They must once — before they built the flyover and the docks — have looked straight out across the Channel to France. The white cliffs loomed above, dangerously close, tinged with mildewy green.

The sun was stronger now and she searched in her bag for her sunglasses. She put them on a little self-consciously, still not certain she'd bought the right pair. They were like the ones she'd seen in photographs of her mother taken in the fifties; heavy plastic frames, dark green lenses.

James would know about his missing car by now. Would he go to work in the Escort? Would he stay at home waiting for her to call?

Along the front there were a number of hotels and she picked one for its old-fashioned net curtains. She was hungry. The front door was open, but the reception area and breakfast room looked deserted. She shifted from one foot to the other and reached down to scratch the side of her knee. With a clatter a girl of about thirteen appeared abruptly from a service door, catching her off guard.

"Can I help you?" She was at the gawky stage where her mind had outpaced her body, and seemed uncomfortably aware of her blotchy complexion. Her hair was long and untidy, pulled backwards by a series of clips, grips and barrettes. There was a hint of suspicion in her eyes, as if she'd seen too much trouble too soon.

"I don't want to stay — I just wondered if I might be able to have some breakfast?" Fiona felt hopeless, unsure of herself faced with this teenager, this young woman who could almost be her own daughter.

"We don't normally do breakfast for non-residents." She looked over Fiona's shoulder. She paused, as if waiting for her to give up, go away, do anything except stay where she was, being a nuisance.

Then something in her relented and she motioned over to the breakfast room. "I expect I can rustle something up for you though."

"Thank you. Thank you very much."

"Tea or coffee?"

"Oh. Umm ... tea. Tea, please." She wandered into the breakfast room, found a table where she could sit facing the door, and pulled the chair underneath her. The tablecloth was heavy and expensive, but there were some old stains on it which weren't ever going to come out now. She thought of her aunt in Guildford who'd always had perfectly starched cloths and napkins, how she'd always served tea from a silver pot into the best china. Was that really twenty-five years ago? She felt an awful pang pass through her, a hopeless sense of regret at not having had children herself, at not having nieces and nephews to treat to afternoon tea. An only child, and it seemed she couldn't have children.

When she was a child she used to look out of the side window of her mother's car as they sped through the countryside, watching the flickering blur of fields and hedgerows — in summer there would be poppies along the edges of cornfields like splashes of red paint — and she would concentrate on not focusing on them; on letting the drifting colours and shapes merge into the whirl of the passing landscape. She would wait, all tensed up, for a rush of birds to burst from the hedge at the sound of the oncoming car and it was impossible not to sigh as they flocked and swirled in great fluid circles across the fields.

She saw with a start the cup of coffee on the table and looked up to find the girl hovering beside her.

"Umm, sorry, what was that?"

The girl tutted, and breathed in a little melodramatically. Fiona could see the irritation in the uplifted chin and raised eyes. The girl repeated her question. "Boiled eggs and toast? Or cereals?"

Fiona looked down at the coffee, the way it had spilled into the saucer. She didn't feel hungry any more.

"I'll have the eggs please. Just one though. Thank you."

The sun was fighting a losing battle to come in through a corner window encrusted with grime and cobwebs. The whole place was run down.

She froze as a man shambled into the room, rubbed his stubbled chin with one hand, and looked around, trying to focus on something elusive. His eyes finally settled on the newspaper on the bar and he shuffled over to it, seemingly unaware of her presence, and scratched the seat of his trousers. He stood there for a moment, swaying very slightly. If he was any closer she'd be able to smell his stale breath, last night's smoke and old alcohol.

Fiona found herself fighting back tears. Thoughts of what she should do next flitted in and out of her head like house martins nest-building. Maybe she should just drive home, face the man she was married to, try to talk it out. But she couldn't drive back, not now, not with the awful rush-hour traffic, stopping and starting through south-east London like some nightmare train shunting half way across the city. But she couldn't go on, either.

She didn't feel free or reckless anymore, not now that she was on England's corner, facing outwards. She felt guilty and resentful and sad, all at the same time. James was a reasonable man, wasn't he? And he would be worried, wouldn't he? And not just because of his precious BMW. A small wash of tenderness run through her. He was just a small boy. It was absurd really, especially when she thought of James's bulk, his bear-like 6'3", his huge hands.

And she hadn't come away simply to go scurrying back like a frightened mouse at the first obstacle she reached. But it all seemed so oppressive and complicated, pressures she could feel in her neck muscles and on the sides of her temples. She wondered whether there was any Paracetamol in the car. Was it the sort of thing James would carry with him? She should ask him. She should know.

The man was staring at her, she realised. The newspaper was half-raised in his arm, perhaps as a form of greeting. She nodded in a way that could be taken as talking to herself. He shook his head vaguely and meandered out of the room.

Where was her breakfast? She looked down and there it was, an egg in a plain white egg-cup, four slices of toast, cut diagonally and stacked in a worn silver rack with dark shadows between the slots. She hadn't seen the girl come and go.

The egg was practically cold and as the first gelatinous spoonful touched the roof of her mouth she thought she might be sick. She felt a small spasm in her stomach and her throat contracting uncomfortably. She pushed the egg to one side and reached for a slice of toast. It was cold. She spread it with some soft butter and a small spoonful of congealed marmalade from a scallop-shaped glass dish, and bit into it, more reluctant to eat now than ever. She seemed to be having trouble chewing, swallowing, and ended up washing the whole sticky mess down with a gulp of tepid coffee. Hadn't she ordered tea?

She had to do something. She couldn't just sit in this hotel all day eating cold food and feeling sick and waiting for something to happen. She caught glimpses of the girl walking back and forth through the hall, and made ineffectual gestures at her for the bill. Eventually she gave up, brushed the crumbs off her skirt, and left the breakfast room.

She paid uncomplainingly, although it seemed expensive. She could afford it — or James could afford it. She discreetly counted the money left in her purse; a little over fifty pounds. She would need more if she was going far. And the car needed petrol already. But she had James's duplicate credit cards, and they would take her a long way — if she wanted to go a long way.

She adjusted her sunglasses in the front porch of the hotel and stepped out onto the pavement. At the end of the street there was a path running up towards the top of the cliff. On her way she saw that one of the houses was a tiny newsagent's which looked as if all the stock from a normal shop had been crammed into somebody's front room. She bought a newspaper, and glanced over the front page. Nothing but trouble; trouble in the Soviet Union; trouble in the Middle East; a continuing recession in the West. She hardly ever read the newspapers. She wondered what James would think. She looked at her watch; he should be at work by now.

The path worked its way steeply up a grassy slope and she was glad of her sensible shoes. The grass was worn away leaving white chalk scars interlaced all the way up the hillside. She could look down into the Eastern Docks now, and out across the still water inside the breakwaters to the sea beyond. She thought she could see France.

A hovercraft was approaching, speeding along the water and leaving a long misty trail behind it. It made her think of the water boatmen she'd seen on stagnant ponds on nature trails. She would crouch down attentively in the quiet woods, watching the little insects skitting along the surface, marvelling at the intricacies of life.

She was hot now, but she pushed on up the hill. Where the path was cut into a shelf from the cliff there was a curious set of rusted iron railings running alongside for fifty yards or so and she wondered what their purpose had been. The lowest of them was about five feet off the ground and she could easily have stepped under it, and out over the cliff-edge. Maybe they had been used for something when they were building the defensive bunkers along here during the war. There were still traces of long-abandoned gun emplacements and slabs of cracked concrete at odd angles in the cliff-face.

Now she was higher up, near the top of the cliffs, she could see the coast of France clearly. It felt like days ago, weeks, since she had left London.

There was a surprising amount of traffic out to sea. Where the ferries had turned on their way into harbour, huge marks were left on the surface, even long after the ship had docked. It was as if they left real tracks in the water.

She watched the lines of cars being fed onto a ferry in an orderly way by four or five men with bright orange jackets. People seemed so meek and trusting, so confident that these semi-uniformed men would deliver them safely to France — yet only a few months before one of the same ferries had gone down near Belgium with its doors still open at sea. But she was sure she would follow the car in front into the belly of the ship, stop where she was told, listen to the instructions about muster stations and life-jackets and forget them immediately.

But she didn't feel like going to France at all. What would she tell James? Maybe she should call someone — her mother? Jill from the tennis club? But no, she would have to keep this mess to herself. She would be found out anyway, or at least suspected. She would have to tell him the truth.

The truth? That she couldn't stand living in the same house, sleeping in the same bed, as the man she had married fourteen years ago? That wasn't right, but when she left this morning, so ashamed and afraid and full of hate, she did mean something like that. What was she saying? That things must change, James. But it sounded so weak, even to her, so petulant. But things would have to change.

She wanted him to receive a letter or a postcard from somewhere far away, for him to have the time not to get emotional about it, but it would never work. He would stand there in the doorway brandishing the letter in one hand, face red and eyes hurt, accusing and questioning. She could see it.

She walked on in silence, staring with unseeing eyes. There had to be a way. She should invite him out to dinner, of course. It was so obvious she didn't know why she hadn't thought of it before. She turned back abruptly and started walking down towards the town. She would telephone him, try and arrange something.

Feeling lighter, she smiled at a man in his sixties breathlessly pursuing a spaniel up the hill. Yes, she would call him.

She walked down into the docks to look for a telephone, and found herself in the departures hall. People queued impatiently for tickets. Everywhere there were small groups of teenagers sitting on their rucksacks, striking up superficial friendships that would barely make it across the Channel. She felt vaguely jealous, but even when she'd been their age it wasn't the kind of travelling she'd wanted to do. She'd been born at the wrong time, or more likely brought up in the wrong family. Yet her cousins had gone off like that, with practically no money and not much more sense of where they were going. Provence. Somewhere near Madrid. Andalucia.

Fiona was different — she'd always wanted to be taken on a Grand Tour, to be chaperoned around the great art capitals of Europe and fall in love with someone inappropriate in Florence. She'd probably read too much Forster. But she'd been born too late for a Grand Tour, and when she and James had finally visited Florence (in the BMW, staying in a restored Tuscan farmhouse belonging to one of James's partners) she'd found it crowded and polluted and noisy. She hadn't even been inside the Uffizi, unable to face the two-hour queue or the crowds she imagined in front of each of the row upon row of ancient canvasses. Instead she'd bought a massive colour guidebook to the museum, and sat in the garden examining its illustrations minutely as if they could provide some sort of answer. James went and visited everything she wanted to see, and returned each evening with boyish tales recounted with a hint of petulance.

She rummaged through her purse until she found a phonecard, and queued to use the callbox. At home the phone rang and rang, and she had a clear mental picture of the hall with the telephone sitting on its table, of how it would sound from the empty bedrooms upstairs, of how it would be ringing and ringing through the house. She made a ghost-like tour, room by room, and was startled by someone tapping her on the shoulder. It was a harassed looking man with a beard; in his forties, anxious eyes. "Ah, excuse me, but are you going to be long? I have to make a call before my ferry leaves." He looked meaningfully at his watch.

She hung up the receiver and recovered the phonecard as the machine spat it out. "No, no. Sorry." She must have been dreaming.

She vaguely heard the man talking to someone a long way away. He looked like someone who would be calling his mother. "Yes, yes, we're fine. The ferry's off in a short while... yes... yes, I will... no... Yes, of course I will... Yes, all right... ah, I have to go now... yes, take care of yourself... bye."

He nodded at her as he hung up, and hurried off to rejoin his family. She stepped back under the grey metal hood and found his phonecard still in the slot. She hesitated for a moment and then pushed it in and tried James's office.

"Waterson, Jones and Scott. Can I help you?" came the receptionist's voice, dulled and tired already by mid-morning.

"I'd like to speak to James Foxton please."

"I'll put you through to his secretary."

There was a pause while she was subjected to a dose of badly recorded classical music. Why did they do that? Was anybody ever reassured or encouraged by this? It was probably one of those ideas that had come across from America and somehow stuck.

"Hello. Can I help you?"

"Ah, yes, hello. I'd like to speak to James Foxton."

"Who's calling please?"

"Oh, it's his wife."

There was a small hesitation. Something was wrong.

"Mrs. Foxton? — Mr. Foxton called in about an hour ago and said he was working at home today. He won't be in today." There was something awful and final about the way she said it.

Fiona felt herself blushing in the callbox, painfully aware that she was about to become the subject of office gossip. "Ah yes, of course. I'd forgotten. Umm, I'm not at home you see," she said, feeling more and more stupid by the second.

All her decision and resolve was gone.

She walked back to the car, her head all crowded and stuffy with unshed tears. There was a piece of paper taped to the driver's side window saying 'Warden — please ticket this car — Resident's Parking Only,' but there was no parking ticket. She peeled the message carefully off and got into the car. She blew her nose, and looked at herself in the mirror. She stared at her impenetrable reflection hopelessly for a while before reversing cautiously out of the dead-end street.

She drove straight home, stopping only for petrol, and parked the car outside, on the road. The weather had changed, the early light gone forever. It was a day like any other, the London sky even and drab, vaguely luminescent. She looked across at the house and saw that the garage was still closed.

In the mirror in her compact she still looked crumpled, deflated. She tried to tidy herself up a little, but it didn't seem to work. She wondered if James was watching her.

She walked up to the front door and rang the bell. Nothing. She fished her keys out of her bag. The house looked like it had been long-abandoned. But as soon as she was inside she saw James standing against the sink in the kitchen, his back to the wall units, arms folded across his chest.

She screamed and pulled her arms up to protect her face. He had a flat, serious expression. She shut her eyes and swayed, reached out a hand to steady herself on the doorframe.

"Oh, God, James. You gave me such a fright. I'm sorry." She felt flushed and frightened still — he hadn't moved.

He stood there, looking at her, his eyes moving up and down very slightly. She had to move now, now or never. It was her move. She took deep breaths, tried to calm herself down, to settle her heart.

"James, I'm not feeling very well."

He nodded, almost imperceptibly, unfolded his arms, and placed his hands behind him on the edge of the sink. She moved towards him, opening her palms towards him, facing those eyes. It was like a well-rehearsed scene from a nightmare. She stopped, still a few feet from him. "James," she wanted to say, "I want to come home."

James held out a hand towards her and she started offering her hand to him in reciprocation. "Car keys," he said, curtly. She looked around her, lost for a moment. Where was her handbag? She saw it in the hall, on the floor. "In my bag." She gestured down at it, said the words thoughtlessly, automatically.

He pushed past her and out of the room, and picked up the bag, rifling through its contents until he found the keys. "I'm going to the office now. I'll talk to you later, Fiona."

He pulled open the door, walked out and down to the road. She watched him as he stepped into the car. He gunned up the engine, revved hard and drove away.

She sat down at the kitchen table and put her head in her hands.

The Canadian

Piers Letcher

I'd been talking to some construction workers in an all night diner, checking out the chances of summer work, and I guess I must have let the time go by. I left with only ten minutes to spare, and I thought I was going to miss the train — no joke as 'The Canadian' only runs every two days out of Toronto — but I was lucky and it was late leaving, and I found a good seat right down the end of one of the cars.

I tried to talk to the pair in the seats across the aisle — even offered them a beer — but it wasn't going anywhere. They were an unusual couple to be traveling together; a pretty, round-faced German girl, about eighteen, and this tight-lipped Brit, maybe thirty-five. Every time I asked them a question they looked at each other first — like I was a bum — before giving me a one word answer. They were both going out all the way to Vancouver, four days and five nights away, but that was the last I saw of them — by the time the train was on its way and I'd come back to my seat they'd moved up the train, found themselves somewhere else to sit, out of range I guess.

Before we even started there was an announcement about how the bar wouldn't be open until morning, so I couldn't even get any extra supplies. I went up to the observation car anyway, to see if I couldn't find some company.

The upstairs section of the car, the domed part, was empty, but downstairs there was a woman sitting on her own at the corner table.

I sat across from her, at the next table, and pulled a beer from my pocket. I ripped off the ringpull, and offered it to her. She looked across at me, and searched my face for something — but accepted anyway, and reached out a hand for the drink. I opened up my beer and we didn't say anything for a while, either of us, and sat there in the near dark of the train station. I guess we were both waiting for the train to start out on its long haul across the country.

She was past her best, definitely. Fortyish, hips widening out but crammed into tight blue jeans, and a baggy white shirt that hid her breasts and was probably meant to. She had deep lines around her eyes which hadn't come from laughing too much, and a neck that looked like pretty soon it'd be wrinkled up like lizard skin. But I'm not so much of a catch myself. I may keep fit, but I look tired, with dark patches under my eyes, and I don't dress so good. I always tell myself it would be different if there was a woman around. I wear a baseball cap like a permanent fixture since my hair started falling out — always used to be a Chicago White Sox cap, but recently I'd started wearing whatever was local; you meet more people that way.

The train gave a little start as we pulled away from the station and made short wheezing noises like an old man who smokes too much as we picked up speed. The lights snapped on when we slipped into the tunnel that runs out under the city, and I looked across at the woman and raised my can to her. "Here's to the journey, huh?" I took a slug of beer and swallowed it slowly. "Here's to the next few nights."

She looked right back at me with eyes that had seen some rough times somewhere down the line, but somehow stayed pretty all the same. She sipped at her beer and said "Thanks." She waited while one of the guards walked slowly through the car counting ticket stubs. "How far down the track you going?" she asked. Her voice was kind of soft, a bit bruised maybe. She had the kind of accent that made me think of the Midwest somewhere, or Country and Western songs, but she was definitely Canadian not American.

"Edmonton," I said, "Yourself?"

She nodded. "Edmonton. My daughter lives out there — well, she's sick out there right now. I'm gonna visit with her in the hospital." She put out a hand and introduced herself, like she'd made up her mind. "Here, I'm Alice. Thanks for the beer."

I moved across to her table and shook her hand. "Joe." I smiled at her. "You're welcome."

It's easy to meet people in trains, easy to start something up. You know it's going to be easy to end it when you step off at the other end and walk out of their lives. I guess she was thinking the same thing. When people want to get real serious they always lay down the ground rules first — they make it clear just what they're giving up, and what they're going to hold back, who gets which night of the week out, and who gets to do the dishes; and they always take it more slowly. But when you meet someone on a train or on the road you get everything, just for a short while. No complications, nothing to live up to.

We finished off the beers and I offered her a pull at the flask. It was Canadian whisky, rye, and she grimaced at the taste. But she didn't run off, and the second time I offered she didn't even make a face, either, so I guessed things were Ok. We stayed there a while, the engine pulling the train through the night, moving west to places I couldn't even put on the map. We talked about nothing special, about the season maybe, about the trouble finding work these days; we were on the same track all the way along.

Eventually she asked me where I was sitting. I pointed down the train, and she gave me a small smile, like she wasn't quite used to it. We turned out to have seats in the same car, but she'd ended up jammed up against some reptile couple from Winnipeg, and I had four seats to myself. She went and fetched her bag from down the corridor and came and sat beside me. She looked across, out the window, and said, "Nothing much to see for the next few hours, anyway."

We sat side by side, facing back down the car, and I don't know whether it was her moving to me or me moving to her but it seemed like no time had passed before we were leaning against each other. She felt warm through my shirt, and after a while I put an arm around her shoulders. I could feel her breath on my neck when I did that, soft like the evening wind off Lake Michigan at the end of summer. I pulled the top off another beer and we shared it slowly, not saying so much, just taking in some good human warmth. After a while she moved a bit and turned to look me in the eyes. "You got family in Edmonton?" She had a pretty speckled gray colour in her eyes that I hadn't noticed before. I guess you could only see it when you got in close.

I didn't answer at first — I was looking into her eyes but thinking of Neil, and why he'd done it. How I probably wasn't even going to find out about it now. Eventually I said slowly, "I did have. My brother used to live out there."

That was all I could say, really. I didn't want to go into the big explanations — how we'd been so close as kids. How he'd ended up in Canada after dodging the draft. How I'd gone to Vietnam anyway, and we'd fallen out, and how when I came back I could see he'd been right all along — a whole generation of kids our age, screwed up for good. But I'd survived somehow and he hadn't, and I was on a train to see what he'd left behind him, and it wasn't going to be much — no wife, no kids, same as me. They'd even repossessed his house; said he'd been way behind on the payments when he killed himself.

Alice must have seen something in the way I'd gone quiet, maybe in my eyes or in my voice, because she touched my shoulder, twice, just softly. And when I looked down into her eyes she turned and leaned her head against my neck. I smelled her hair, and touched her arm, and tried not to think about Neil the way I'd read about him in the coroner's report, lying in a bloodstained bathroom, half his face blown off by a 12-gauge.

I let my fingers move slowly up and down, first along Alice's arm and then on her side where I could feel the outward swell of her breast, and all the time I kept breathing in the dry summer-straw smell of her hair and after a while she nuzzled up to my neck and sighed.

The night stretched out in front of us and it felt like we were on the way to nowhere, safe somehow in the train, safe for a while at least, cut off from the outside world. She kissed my neck, and I bent down to kiss her face. She tasted of railway stations, of tiredness and spoiled dreams. The lights were off for the night and it was strange kissing her in the dark with all those people nearby, sleeping as best they could in the narrow seats, and Ontario rushing by in the night. There was some kind of problem with the heating control — I guess they couldn't shut it off — and we were both sweating in the dark. She had her hand inside my shirt and was touching my chest, and I stroked her breasts underneath her blouse.

It felt like it must have been a long time for both of us. We went into one of the cramped little washrooms they have at the end of each car, and we fucked in there with the train rattling across the dark landscape and the heaters pumping hot air along the stuffy corridors. We clung to each other afterwards in that isolated little room like drunks, sweaty and gasping and laughing at the strangeness of it, and it wasn't like it sometimes is where as soon as it's over you feel cold and disgusted. It was close, and intimate, and maybe more than that.

I left Alice in there tidying herself up and went back to our seats. The car looked just like it had a half hour before, the same sprawled figures across the seats, the same night noises. The air was heavy and sweaty and smelled of stale blankets and old shoes. People's faces had gone waxy in the heat.

It didn't feel like I slept, but I must have because the night went by faster than I expected. By the time it was light I was stiff and my arm had gone dead where Alice was sleeping on it. We stayed like that, slumped together, until the train stopped. Alice went off and changed into a fresh blouse with frills down the front, and came back looking younger somehow, less tired. We were stopped at some nowhere station in a clearing in the forests and she went to look for coffee, leaving me trying to piece together the night somehow and wondering where all this was going.

I took off my cap and looked at the new season Toronto Blue Jays design. I scratched my scalp and wondered how they did the stitching. There must be some kind of machine to do it I guess.

I stood up to stretch, tired suddenly, and saw Alice waving at me from outside, so I walked stiffly along to the exit door and climbed down beside the train. Small clouds of steam were condensing in the early sunlight and I found myself liking this forgettable little place stranded miles from anywhere, knowing I'd probably never come back this way again. She handed me a cup and we stood there together, saying nothing, sipping at the boiling coffee, staring down the track into the morning-orange light. The drinks steamed and the rails stretched away, gleaming in the sunlight.

Over the next two nights we broke all the rules, or at least she did. She told me everything. She told me about her husband and the little daughter she'd left in smalltown Alberta ten years before, about the little souvenir shop she ran at Niagara Falls, about her daughter's illness; she told me everything. I don't recall how it started, but it seemed that what she really wanted, even more than the warmth and the arm around her shoulders, was someone to listen to her. I don't normally listen so good, but her story reached me, touched me somewhere deep inside. I told her about Neil, too, and she said she knew. She'd known something like that had happened.

We arrived in Edmonton on a freezing morning after three nights on the train, restless after being confined so long to the same small area, eyes itching. It was like we'd moved back a whole season from Toronto — spring was almost turning to summer over there; but here there were still piles of old snow everywhere. The sky was heavy as hell and you could see little ice-crystals swirling in the floodlights of the station with a hint of dawn over to the east. There was a whole crew at the front of the train trying to fit on a snow-plow; a couple of guys in uniform were talking about fresh falls of snow up in Jasper. Something about the morning made me want to stay on the train all the way across the mountains to Vancouver and the ocean. There didn't seem to be anything to keep me in Edmonton now, not really, not any more. But there was still one thing.

We stood in the bright underground lobby trying to think of easy things to say. Alice went over to the drinks counter and came back with a glass of juice and a coffee for each of us and I could see she must have done some waitressing sometime from the way she carried it all back so neatly. She handed me my drinks, put hers down on a shelf and started writing an address on the paper serviette. The felt tip she was using made blotchy stains right through the paper. She handed it to me with a small smile like the one she'd first given me, back when I first saw her in the observation car on the train in Toronto. "Well, Joe." She hesitated. "Well, if you're ever in Niagara Falls..."

"Thanks." I looked at the address. "Thanks." I folded up the tissue and put it in my jeans pocket. We stood there drinking coffee and it took me a while to realise she was waiting for something from me too. "Look, I'm sorry, Alice. I don't have any forwarding address right now." I stopped, shrugged my shoulders a little. "But I'll write when I've got things sorted out, Ok?"

She looked into my eyes, as if searching for something I wasn't quite saying, and then nodded a couple of times, just short nods like she was trying to convince herself. She collected up the cups, found a trash can to throw them in, and came back tucking in the sides of her shirt with her thumbs. She extended her hand in a kind of formal goodbye, so I took it and pulled her to me, hugged her tight. We kissed that one last time, and she gave me a big wide smile. She said "Well, I guess we can't stand here all day," but she made it sound like a question, and I wanted to say "Why not?" but I just nodded like a fool, and she picked up her bags and walked away into the crowd by the door, off to look for her bus. I could picture her headed down a deserted farm road, the grain stores like cathedrals in the empty fields, the skies gray and unending above her. She'd said she had to go. She had to go and see her husband first. Her ex-husband.

I found the hospital easily enough; Edmonton's not so big. The doctors were pretty suspicious at first — I guess they have to be when you think about it — but once I told them about knowing Alice one of them explained to me about the operation her daughter Cathy needed. I didn't really understand the details too well, but I knew as good as anyone else how much health care costs, so I asked the doctor if the money was all there. "That's the thing," he said, shaking his head slowly. "The family can't pay, so she's still on the waiting list." He hurried on, almost embarrassed. "Obviously if her situation gets any worse we'll have her in for surgery right away, but she's stable right now, so there's nothing we can do really." He sounded as if he knew it was an excuse. I looked at his well-shaven profile, his well-clipped fingernails, his spotless shirt and tie.

I wrote out a check to the hospital, anyway, and he looked over it professionally. It was just about all the money I had left over from being made redundant in Detroit. It didn't matter. He stood up from behind his desk and I could see it was time to go. He looked down at my sneakers and then up at my hat, just avoiding looking me in the eye. "I'm sure Cathy'll be on her feet in no time." It didn't sound like he believed it himself. He stared over my shoulder. "Is there anywhere we can reach you, ..." he looked down at the check he was still holding, and read my name, "... Mr. Miller?" I shook my head. "It's Ok. I'll find out from Alice." I wanted to see Cathy, I wanted to see what kind of daughter Alice would have had, but something stopped me. It wouldn't have been right, somehow.

He reached out and gave me a firm, dry handshake with one hand while ushering me out of his office with the other. I felt about fifteen years old. As we parted he said, "You take care now," and he watched me walk down the corridor and maybe counted to five before shutting the door.

It's funny, you do something like that and you expect to feel big about it, like the world owes you something. But going down in the elevator all I felt was a kind of sadness, almost a sense of disappointment. I thought I should feel different about it. Maybe it's always like that when you do something big for the first time. I don't know.

I stood outside the hospital, hands in my pockets, looking for any irregularities in the flat gray sky, wondering what I was going to do. A nurse coming out of the building, on her way home from the night shift I guess, ran into me as she came out through the sliding doors. She asked me if I was Ok. I nodded, said I was just getting a breath of fresh air. And she said "Sure?" and I nodded again and she walked over to a beat-up station wagon in the parking lot. I watched her drive off, remembering the tiredness you only get after a long, long shift, and envied her for a moment.

After all that I could see it would be pointless trying to find out any more about Neil. There wasn't going to be any of his stuff left out there anyway, and there wasn't going to be anyone who could help me find out. I was going to have to live with that. There wasn't anything to do. I'd come a long way to find that out, too, three quarters of the way across the country. And I had to get a job now; I was more or less flat broke. I thought about it. Maybe I could get a bus out west before the next train in two days time.

In the bar at the Greyhound Terminal there were some guys in heavy work shirts standing in a small group together, so I picked a barstool near enough to listen. Two of them had been out in British Columbia, tree planting, the previous season, it seemed, and they were on their way back out there. I joined in the conversation and it sounded like good work, so I asked if I could tag along. A couple of the younger guys joined in, and we all went over together to a table and had a couple more beers. Later on we all caught the night bus out to Vancouver. They were hiring now, they said, and it seemed like it was one of those jobs anyone could do.

Planting out those trees in Canada was as hard a job as I ever did. But there was a real sense of achievement to it — not like building automobiles or working in construction — there was a sense of maybe helping nature along a little bit. I wrote Alice and told her that. And I said right at the end that maybe after the summer, when I'd saved up some money, I'd come and see her in Niagara Falls.

Long Skirts and Worse
Piers Letcher

It was one of those smart restaurants in the West End that seems almost silent. Deep pile carpets, subdued lighting, candles in jars on the tables, deferential waiters. It was spoiled a little for Mark because he'd once worked in the kitchen of a restaurant just like this one. He knew all about the clamour, the grease and the dirt you found backstage in even the most luxurious establishment.

Jo-Ann smiled up at him over a forkful of Radicchio. Blonde, clear-eyed, Australian. Young, intelligent, and at his table. And she wanted him. He was sure of that now.

He'd collected her from her flat off Westbourne Grove, and she'd asked him in for an aperitif. She'd served over-chilled wine into long-stemmed glasses and chattered in her cheerful way about some incident that had amused her on the way home on the underground.

He'd fallen for her on the very first day she'd started work. The way she'd flung open the windows letting in all the City sounds; the traffic far below, the distant sirens, the bells of the City churches. Oranges and Lemons. She'd been brought in on a three month contract supporting some of the software development — not on his project, but he'd found ways of being near her. She wasn't short of friends or would-be friends in the office but she seemed to know few people outside. London was like that. Much harder to meet people than you'd think. He remembered when he'd first come up to town and he'd thought he'd have too many people to know, too many things to see and do. And then he'd spent the first three months in that awful bedsit in the Caledonian Road.

She'd sat down on the sofa opposite and drawn her knees up, cradling her shins in her arms, her long skirt pressed against her legs, bare feet pointing almost demurely like a ballet dancer's. She sipped slowly at her wine and each time her skirt slid across a little further, revealing a little more of her inner leg. He sat in the chair opposite, transfixed, wide-eyed, unable to take his eyes off her. He told himself off. You're not a kid, Mark, you don't have to be excited by that kind of thing. But he couldn't help it. Any moment now he would see her knickers. He'd be ready to bet on plain white, no frills. She paused in the middle of a story about her first week in London, about how she'd been horrified by the Earl's Court Road, by the dirt and filth everywhere, and took another sip of her wine. She twirled the glass by its stem and her skirt slipped away a fraction more. He could see the bottom of her blouse where it was tucked in now. But that wasn't what shocked him. What shocked him was that she wasn't wearing any knickers. He couldn't believe it.

She was smiling at him, moving off the sofa to collect his glass, to offer him a refill. He nodded, embarrassed to find himself aroused and breathless. Part of him was unbearably excited. But a small voice at the back of his mind was busy condemning her.

They drank the second glass more quickly and the alcohol went straight to his head. In the car on the way to the restaurant he kept looking down at the shape of her legs through her skirt. He let his imagination do the touching. He reddened when she looked across at him while they were waiting to filter into the traffic going around Marble Arch.

The restaurant was a fraction too warm. Or maybe it was because he was so aroused. She was delicious. She was his. Her eyes lit up in the candle glow as she told him about her grandmother who'd been brought up at the turn of the century, somewhere on Australia's West Coast.

"You can't imagine it now, but they had to be entirely self-sufficient then. They even had to make their own soap. Can you imagine that? Even now it's a pretty wild place. You can drive for a day and a half and not see anyone."

Australians seemed to love Australia. They seemed to have it deep inside them, constantly missed, held up as the yardstick against which everything else was judged. But anywhere you went, all around the world, you'd find Australians. More Australians than Americans, even. If Australia was so wonderful why didn't they stay there?

Two waiters arrived bearing large oval plates with silver covers. With a flourish they uncovered the dishes to reveal mouth-watering slivers of red mullet interspersed with crayfish tails. Strategically placed around the edge were tiny mounds of vegetables — spinach, red cabbage, and gratin dauphinois.

The first time he'd asked Jo-Ann out he'd been more nervous than a sixteen year old. She'd seemed so confident, so self-assured. And flirtatious in a slightly forbidding way. She seemed to be able to deflect all advances while giving the impression that she was a soft touch. He couldn't believe it when she'd accepted, and he'd spent the whole afternoon wandering around the office puffed up like a penguin.

They'd gone out to a wine bar far enough from the office that they wouldn't find any of the people they worked with. The bottle of Graves Blanc Sec had disappeared all too quickly between them, three glasses apiece, and she'd refused a second, or even another half. She stood up and thanked him and said that she'd have to get back. As if she had someone to go back to. As if she didn't live alone.

He'd been almost silent as they walked along to the underground station, full of thoughts of riding all the way out west with her, of carrying her satchel home. At the entrance she'd held out her hand to shake his, to smile and to thank him, but what he'd wanted was a kiss. He smiled back at her woefully, bitterness clouding in on him. Rattling his way home on the Northern line he'd been submerged by waves of desperation.

The next time she'd let him come back with her to her flat. He'd walked up the stairs to the first floor behind her, hypnotised by the swish of her long black skirt, expecting nothing, expecting it all. And then she'd turned to him on the landing, her key already in the lock, and said "Goodnight, Mark. Thanks for a lovely evening, and thanks for walking me home." And she'd disappeared indoors, the door latching shut behind her. He'd stood outside on the street watching her window, imagining her at the kitchen sink filling up a kettle. Imagining her getting undressed, washing carefully, brushing her teeth. He'd imagined her sliding between pale sheets, checking the setting on the alarm clock. He'd imagined it all.

He poured the last of the Chambolle-Musigny into their glasses as she told him about a whale she'd discovered once stranded on a remote beach. She laughed as she said that you could smell the rotting hulk for miles and miles downwind. She wrinkled her nose up at him, and tilted her head to one side. He wanted her, badly.

He told her about the only whales he'd ever seen, on the Whale Watch he'd been on in Maine. The giant creatures surfaced surprisingly fast, silky smooth and vast, and rode the waves alongside the boat for a few seconds before blowing evil-smelling spray from their blowholes. "Which only goes to prove that whales also have bad breath," he closed, as a waiter arrived to clear away the remains of his Magret de Canard and her veal. He was intoxicated by her, he was hot under the collar, excited by her. He didn't know much about love, but he knew what he wanted.

Things were going well this time. Normally he didn't have much luck with women but this time he knew things were right. She was as hot for it as he was. He could tell. He'd known it from the last time he'd seen her, at her place.

He'd been invited to a reciprocal supper with her, following the virtuoso Chinese meal he'd created for her at his flat. He'd tempted himself with visions of the culinary extravaganzas she might come up with, but as it turned out the food was plain; traditional Italian. He didn't care — she'd sparkled in front of him, taken his breath away. He could just watch her, just listen to her talk. He thought of her as his golden girl, as his own private source of sunshine.

She'd disappeared into the kitchen with the rest of the dishes and had started fixing coffee, leaving him alone with a wall full of bookshelves. They were full of good literature, art books and serious theses, and he didn't know whether to be surprised or whether indeed these were her books. He pulled a coffee table book from a low shelf and found it was a collection of Australian fashion designs from five years before. On the inside cover there was a scribbled dedication to "Jo-Ann, the tops", with "p.47!" written underneath in a heavy hand. He turned to the page and was astonished to see a picture of Jo-Ann draped across a fallen log in a virgin forest wearing nothing but a multi-coloured scarf around her waist. Her hair fell across her face and she looked deliciously abandoned, her breasts young and firm, her neck long and defenceless. He shut the book hastily as he heard the coffee cups clattering on the tray and slid the book back into the bookshelf just in time.

The sorbets had been exquisite, the coffee and chocolates perfect. The bill, of course, was enormous, but his credit card softened the blow a little. And it was a good investment, anyway. He sighed to himself in anticipation of the events ahead. Jo-Ann came back from the Ladies and brushed his shoulder with her hand as she sat down. It was now or never.

"Can I ask you something, Jo-Ann?"

"Yes, of course."

"Something personal?"

She looked at him coyly. Had she guessed? She nodded at him, flashed those even teeth at him. "Go on then."

"Why aren't you wearing anything under your skirt?"

The pause seemed to last forever. She narrowed her eyes, frowned, looked down at the heavy linen tablecloth. He'd made it. She hadn't reacted fast enough. She made the faintest of smiles at him, and looked from side to side like someone trapped. She started to stand up and he stood up slowly himself.

The slap was the last thing he'd expected. He was knocked sideways by the force of it. As he slipped he grabbed at the edge of the tablecloth and the last two glasses on the table fell over, red wine spreading in an ugly stain from hers. He couldn't believe it. Where had he gone wrong? She'd been leading him along all the time. She pushed past him and was gone.

His vision wasn't working properly. He could feel the imprint of her fingers on his face, glowing red, burning. At the few tables still occupied nobody had turned around, no-one was looking his way. Thank God he was in England. It was as if nothing had happened. It was as though he had just stood up from his meal having eaten alone. He'd have to rush to catch her. She'd be heading for the underground or the taxi rank on Shaftesbury Avenue.

He caught one of the waiters smirking as he flew out of the door and regretted momentarily that there wasn't going to be time to both punch him and catch Jo-Ann. He was furious. With himself as well as her. She was the tart. She was the one who was ready to pose half-naked for Australian photographers. He'd only said the truth, hadn't he? He caught sight of her turning the corner onto Old Compton Street and sprinted to catch her.

As he approached she heard him coming and whirled round to face him. He wasn't expecting her to stand her ground and skidded to a halt on his expensive leather-soled shoes, breathless.

"You fucking shit, Mark. You stay away from me!"

"Jo-Ann, you don't understand..."

It was all too late. She was walking away, brisk and determined, into the crowds on Shaftesbury Avenue. He felt himself shaking impotently. She was just another bloody tease. No wonder nobody at work had managed to get off with her. Cow. No bloody wonder she was single.

He looked up at a streetlight and the first single spatter of rain caught him in the eye. Blinking in frustration he put up a hand to wipe it away and was surprised by how much his cheek still stung. He hadn't even got a bloody umbrella. She would be in a taxi by now, or on the westbound platform of the Central line. The rain started coming down in gobbets, plastering his thinning hair to his skull. Dirty rain, dirty city.

Settling In

Lynn Haroutian

See, I'm new in town, and it takes me a few days to find the laundromat and by then I'm irritated 'cause I feel like I'm never going to get everything into my new place and it's been raining all week and it's raining again and I do so enjoy lugging a basket full of dirty clothes around in the rain.

But I find the laundromat and figure out how to work the machine that changes dollar bills and how to put the detergent in before the clothes and when the rinse cycle starts so I can add fabric softener at the right time. And I say hello to the guy who runs this place, he's real friendly and he's very proud of his laundromat, he's got these signs all over, like 'Fan For Use of Customers, Please be Considerate of Your Neighbors' and 'Static Control Sheets For Your Use' and 'Start Dryer With One Quarter Then Add More Later as Needed', real helpful.

So we're talking about what it will cost to get a jacket dry cleaned, he does dry cleaning on the side, and my clothes are spinning around in the dryers, one load on the 'Light Permanent Press' cycle and one on the 'Whites and Coloreds' cycle. And I'm kind of, you know, congratulating myself a little, 'cause I'm new here and I've already figured out how to use the laundromat, I got my clothes washed and now they're drying. And it's pretty quiet, just me and José, that's the owner, he's behind the counter with the dry cleaning, and this old guy comes in with two baskets of clothes and he takes over a whole row of washers, and I can see he's only putting one kind of clothes in each machine, like, he puts his shirts in one, his underwear in another, his sheets in another. So each machine winds up with half a load in it, and it costs $1.25 no matter how much you put in, and I figure he's just spent $7.50 for about $3.75 worth of clothes, but that's what he does.

Well this is mildly interesting, but hey, who am I to cast stones, I just figured out how to use the money changer and the washers and dryers today. So I pick up a *Reader's Digest* and start reading and forget about the old guy.

So a little while later, I get up to put another couple of quarters in my dryers, and that's when he starts pacing back and forth along the row of washers. I don't really pay him much attention, I'm just waiting for my 'Light Permanent Press' and my 'Whites and Coloreds' to finish tango-ing in the dryer.

Then he starts, "Dammit, I tol' you to leave me alone. Why won't you leave me alone? I tol' you and TOL' you and TOL' you!"

And as far as I can tell, he's talking to the load of shirts that he's now taking out of washer #4 and folding real carefully.

"Dammit, I tol' you and TOL' you. Why don't you ever lissen to me?"

And he's folding his sheets now, "Why do I havta keep repeatin' myself? Why don't you lissen to me the first time?"

And a few more people come in, an old couple, he's carrying the clothes in a big trash bag and she's got the detergent and fabric softener, and then some young guy who looks like he's just left home and dealing with a laundromat is almost more than he can handle, and some middle-aged woman who smiles and says, "Hi, Emile, how ya doin' today?" to the old guy who's been talking to himself and he stops in mid-tirade and says, "I'm good Carol, how are you?" and they chat for a couple of minutes. Then Carol's got her wash going so she leaves and Emile starts pacing again, and pretty soon he's talking again, "Dammit, I tol' you and TOL' you, no-one ever lissens to me, why won't you lissen to me? Why do I havta keep REPEATIN' myself?"

And the old couple and the young guy are giving these funny looks like maybe they're considering if they can wait another day to do the wash. And this Emile is still pacing and talking up a blue streak.

So now I'm wondering what José's gonna do, being so proud of his place and all, and here's this guy Emile practically driving business away. But José just stands there, with this little smile on his face. So Emile keeps folding his clothes, he's got all the washers empty now and he takes each pile of clothes to a separate dryer, shirts in one, underwear in another, and places the piles inside real careful, like he's putting them away in his bureau or something, and he puts his quarters in and starts up the dryers but he misses one.

So Emile's pacing again and by now my 'Light Permanent Press' and my 'Whites and Coloreds' are done so I'm folding my jeans and ready to go. And José comes over and pushes in the coin holder to start Emile's last dryer, and as he goes by he smiles at me and says, "Sometimes he just needs a little help engaging the mechanism."

So I say, "See you next week, José." and when I get outside the rain's finally stopped.

The Exhibition

Timothy Martin

I am not merely an admirer of Egon Schiele, but a fellow conspirator. He alone is capable of producing on a physical level what I myself can only visualize in vanishing vignettes and askew contortions upon a canvas of the mind. I too battle the beast within, reconcile the silences, linger where shadows collide. Recalcitrant souls, each of us seeking solace in isolation, fellowship in withdrawal, expression through introspection.

Enlightened words of the faithful, you say, but at the Schiele retrospective at the Royal Academy... I heard the crow of the cock.

Even now, the point at which wisdom ran amok escapes me, for my reverence for the exhibition was pure. From the moment I spotted the poster until the opening day, I set the stage, performed the necessary libations.

I can still evoke those sentiments of earnest, those preconceived notions of revelation. The instant I ascertained the true extent and purpose undertaken, my course was certain, ordained and free of deliberation. The Schiele exhibition at the Royal Academy was unique in that it was the most comprehensive and complete mounted to date. A total of 145 paintings and drawings had been prised from the hands of curators and private collectors alike. In addition to the admirable breadth of the collection assembled, a serious attempt was made to place the artist in perspective alongside his Viennese contemporaries. Klimt, Kokoschka, Hofmann and the rest also adorned the walls. In sum, a major event in no circumstances to be missed.

The poster alone conjured up visions.

There lay the vigilant one incubating his stoicism within the confines of a sleeping bag on the steps outside the Academy at 5am. Modesty his credo, he will nevertheless manage to articulate his number at the turnstile in mattter of fact tones to those he presumes inspired by such acts of devotion.

There is the opinionated art critic who has come to shadow any fledgling appreciation she once held at a less discerning point in her career. She is quick to formulate an opinion, to encapsulate a statement, to drop the offbeat; all in an authoritative voice audible to everyone in the room. She's ever ready to concur with the snide remark, to note the inadequate lighting, the harmful humidity levels, the lack of sofas, the slothful security guards. Every exhibition is below standard, another vindication of the feebleness of human expression, another joy twisted at the hands of humiliation.

There is also the two-week connoisseur on her annual pilgrimage to a museum of art. She has waited for a lull in the creative and intellectual impulses undulating in the hamlets to seek a respiteful cultural event that will rekindle the human flame which burns in us all. I call her a two-week connoisseur because that's the length of time exclamations such as, "Very interesting," and, "Oh Sarah, love, you really must go and see it," and one more, "Very interesting," for further accentuation, will enliven dinner parties, get the ball rolling during cocktails and momentarily enrapture a bridge game. It is also the approximate length of time before the catalogue takes flight from the coffee table to the loftier heights on the top shelf between King Tutankhamen and Mrs. Beeton.

And of course there is the aspiring creative genius, in black from head to toe with a three-day scruff of a beard, portfolio strapped over his shoulder, and paint-spattered shoes, who always seems to be looking at you, or her, or any new face that comes into the room, more than the works hanging on the walls. Such longing in such a setting makes one ponder the true ambition of this patron. Would he not feel more at home resting his elbow on a wine bar or chilling his fingertips at a local rock venue?

As for myself, I sought to avoid these external stimulations and images, and glide through the rooms uninterrupted, contemplate the works unperturbed along corridors void of baggage. With this resplendent scenario in mind, timing was critical. It was all too easy to imagine the masses swarming through the Academy in the first few weeks of the exhibition so I selected the final day, February 17th, in the hope that the six-week interim would be sufficient to satiate most potential visitors. As for the lethargic ones, or those who had recently fallen off the bus, the early hours of the last day would be acknowledged punctually for fear of missing out on both the exhibition and the heady conversations to follow.

I could therefore set aside the final four hours of the final day for an encounter of my own. For only alone could I come before the emaciated features and hollow eyes as an initiate. Only alone could I parade past the gauntlet of resistance members; a discreet gesticulation to one, a slight nod of the head to another.

Opening day was torture. I didn't need to stroll by the Academy: I could see it in all detail and lucidity from afar. There were the hordes trampling and jostling one another to get in, only to browse and pass through as dispassionately as promenading Lithuanians at Lenin's mausoleum. I could touch the pseudo-afficionados lingering in the doorway and on the steps with their supercilious smiles and feigned concurrences. Here, they uttered clichés as original and recognizable as last month's edition of *Art News*.

No, it was all too much to bear at a distance, much less in person. A desecrating spectacle amusing perhaps to barbarians and philistines, but eliciting little more than disdain on my part.

Throughout the following six weeks, I avoided the critics and tossed aside the third sections. I was not inclined to allow the mainstream to taint the exhibition with their articulate musings and preferred to recline in serene anticipation, oblivious to the gathering clouds. Besides, I had heard the abuse heaped upon Egon on numerous occasions and had come to classify such meanderings under 'uninspired' once and for all. Lewd, perverse, morbid, sick, pornographic, schizophrenic, vulgar. Please. Do we not shudder in the face of such images out of recognition? Alienation, I dare say, wouldn't rupture our composure so intensely and would conjure up very different sentiments. The vehemence and outrage surrounding Schiele's work, wherever it is exhibited, is similar to the cries of defence gasped reflexively by a colleague stepping out of a pornographic cinema. As long as he can hold up another's photograph and proclaim, "deviant," he is exonerated. Yes, the day is a long way off when truth is dislodged from the throat, and a distant one indeed when cathode rays are supplanted by looking glasses.

The morning of the 17th finally arrived after much expectation and resolve. For the umpteenth time, I found myself seated on the edge of the bed, meticulously counting out the correct bus fare and entrance fee. I set my watch and looked up the opening hours of the Academy once again to ensure success. The distant sound of thunder and the darkening skies outside my window brought a smile to my lips; a deluge. Just what was needed to weed out the faint-hearted.

The bus ride gave me time to gain composure, and, my head resting against the window, to allow my imagination to run ahead. I stood freely before *The Truth Was Revealed*, my head tipped to one side, re-examining the painting sideways, even upside down if need be, to discern a revealing angle, an awe-inspiring detail, an allusive, subtle stroke of the brush. I stole through the room, bent down, gripped the floor and pirhouetted around, laughing, to surprise the pageant on the wall opposite...

I suppose my glance appeared rather poised and confident, for upon approaching the Academy I saw no souls whatsoever, either braving the rain or queueing up at the entrance. The only passenger to get off the bus, I splashed through a few puddles, walked up the steps to the front door, purchased a ticket, and entered the foyer to find the entrance hall as I had hoped; empty.

After taking off my overcoat and shaking out my umbrella, I went summarily to the Gents. While straightening my hair and tucking in my shirt-tails, I took a few deep breaths. This was it, the moment I had planned with such unwavering diligence and forethought. Nothing stood between me and the most comprehensive showing of Schiele's work to date.

I entered the first room with hesitation, for fear of discovering a few stragglers waiting for the downpour to subside or the odd 'art student' chatting up a girl. But no. Although I could hear a few muted voices, they seemed to be distant and far removed from the first gallery.

I now stood before the first painting. Eyes closed tightly, I tried to vanquish any residual thoughts or impressions of the outside world. But before my exorcism of the external was complete I was rudely awakened by a girl's laughter. My first reaction was that of sacrilege, but upon hearing a follow-up giggle, I thought, why not? Have I too not laughed at some oblique smirk or painful expectancy of horror? Moreover, the voice was natural and carefree to the point of being utterly oblivious. I looked at the painting and couldn't help sensing a lack of inspiration compared with other works with which I was familiar. Approaching the second canvas, I began to wonder which gallery the voice emanated from. Halted beneath *Death and Girl*, I found myself more expectant of the prospects which lay ahead than contemplative of the painting in front of me. I strode round the gallery at an increasing pace, for now I could clearly hear her footsteps.

I peered into the second gallery and fleetingly caught the contours of the back of her legs as she passed into the room beyond. I walked into the second gallery casually, almost with a step of hesitation. I kept up a comparable pace to her own, always in an adjacent gallery, not wishing to alarm her, my demeanour no more menacing than the average patron. I slowly gained ground to the extent that by the fourth gallery, we were six paintings apart. I didn't dare attempt a manouevre which would afford me a frontal view. A direct glimpse would surely give me away: my lack of self-possession would shed light on my true intentions, my hastc would reverberate with over-zealous interest.

Just as I found her scent lingering in front of *Dead Mother* I began to imagine her as a patron similar to myself. Was she too not here in the final hours? Was she not laughing unselfconsciously and occasionally leaning forward to catch an obscure detail, a change of light? Did she not twirl her skirt effortlessly as she turned on her heels to review a previous sketch or two?

Hesitatingly shifting from painting to painting, I began to grow increasingly anxious and the hands on my watch urged me to relinquish the hunt, cast the girl out of my mind, and resume my natural course of action in the precious little time remaining. But passions failed to subside and, if anything, intensified in obstinate disdain for any reasoning I could concoct. The paintings began to appear redundant, tones veered towards the opaque, themes condensed to juvenile dimensions.

I entered the sixth and final gallery and halted, instantly gripped with fear and anxiety — she was nowhere to be seen. Frantic, I bolted through the room and out into the foyer, finding it painfully silent and omnisciently vacant. I swiftly passed through the exit door and raced down the steps, but there was nothing but emptiness and the click of the door locking behind me.

Race Fever

Melinda Regnell

In 1971, I was standing on the roof of our van in the infield at Watkin's Glenn Speedway in upper-state New York and watched François Severte come out of the ninth turn at about 145 miles per hour and glance off the cement retaining wall. He and his car toppled ass over tea-kettle three times before they both came apart in small pieces.

It rained all weekend that year at the Glenn. The bog party was flooded; the water stopped working in the infield; it was cold.

I haven't thought about that race in years.

I realized last night, that I have spent the better part of about twelve years in and around race tracks with Nils. He doesn't race, (thank God), but his business interests have always had connections to racing. He has always been either a sponsor or a vendor or a member of a pit crew.

I have never really sat in the bleachers. Even at the races where I didn't spend my time sitting on the back of the van selling spark plugs or fan belts, I didn't get to sit in the bleachers. I sat, instead, in race cars, or in tow trucks or push vehicles. There was a time when I knew every modified and super-modified racer in New England by name, and they knew me.

Armand Holly would come over just before each race and chat while his crew warmed up his car. Junior Landry would arrive at the race after his crew had already run the heats for him. He would saunter by the back of the van and get his face-shield washed.

Brought him luck, he would say.

Howard Brown, on the other hand, would walk by and nod a greeting. This was a lot for the 'Old Man'... he didn't talk much to anyone. And Ollie Silver would come by and sit on the back with me and drink a Coke... to calm his nerves. I was never quite sure sure how Coke was going to 'calm' his nerves, but I used to smoke Marlboro and drink ginger ale to clear my throat before going on stage, so who am I to talk?

Ollie was a looker in those days. Six foot two with dark good looks and black hair. He and Junior, along with Armand and the 'Old Man' were the grand old men of racing in those days... and they were all sitting on the back of our truck and talking to me. I was some impressed, let me tell you. More importantly, everyone else was impressed. And that was good for business.

I was secretly in love with Armand. He wasn't the best looking, but there was something behind his eyes that pulled on my heart strings, and I would swoon every time he came by. And while he talked to me, his face would smile, but his eyes were somewhere else, and they did not.

I guess I wanted to cuddle him and make it better. I have learned over and over that this approach does not work unless what you are cuddling is three years old and what you are making better is a scun knee; but that has never prevented me from wanting to, none-the-less.

We would sit and talk about the weather or the racing stats, there on the back of the truck, and then he would pat me on the head and go climb into his race car.

You know, it's funny. I have come very close several times in my life to de-balling that particular sub-species of male that finds it necessary to pat diminutive women on the head like puppies. And, I don't think Armand was that much different from the ones that flirted with becoming sopranos, coming, as he did from a very French, very conservative background. I suspect the difference was that I 'liked' Armand. But I would be careful not to admit that in public. Anyway, I wanted him to win very much, but he never did.

The guys said (when they could be enticed into saying anything about a legend that walked among them) that he was the best there ever was until he ran a young driver into the wall.

Armand spent several months in the hospital recovering from his injuries. He broke his jaw, and several ribs and his hip, and crushed an ankle. They said that when he came out, he was never the same. He didn't run so hard into the corners anymore; he didn't run the outside car up in the turns. He didn't have that 'edge' that got you the checkered flag. They said this was because he was so badly hurt.

I don't know, but I don't think his injuries had anything to do with it. I always thought it had something to do with the fact that the young driver was killed. I don't think he ever wanted to be the 'other driver' ever again.

But, he was my favorite anyway. And when he stopped racing, I missed him very badly.

And, of course, there were the young drivers. The ones who drove the street stocks and chargers. I wouldn't have trusted any one of the cars they drove to get me to the corner store and back, but they'd come coughing and sputtering down pit road every Saturday at 4pm when the pits opened and spend all night beating on those machines to get them to run around the track.

They were our bread and butter customers. The big boys, they came with four sets of tires and an extra engine and enough parts to stock a repair center. Their stops by the truck were of a social, soon-to-be-legendary nature.

The little guys, they were at the back of the truck all night buying this and that to try and make it through the race.

I always wondered about the money they spent. Ollie or Armand, they were lucky if they had a quarter in their pockets. They didn't intend to have to buy anything. Not that they didn't have money, they just didn't carry it to the track.

These other guys, they'd come flash a wad of twenties and start buying.

I asked Nils about it once. He said,

"Thursday is payday."

"Fine, but what do they live on the rest of the week?"

"Sometimes, they win."

"Sometimes, they don't!" He just looked at me. I chalked it up to another little piece of male magic that I would never understand.

Sort of like peacock strutting and tail fluffing... you know?

One night, a woman I didn't recognize came to the back of the truck with her 'driver'. They had three little kids tagging along behind and she carried another on her hip.

"How much for a set of plugs?" the guy asks.

Nils looked up and said, "Sixteen."

This guy looks at the woman and she hands him the kid. She digs in her pockets and comes up with two fives and four ones. They trade the kid back again. He empties his pockets and comes up with one dollar and 69 cents.

Nils handed him the plugs and says, "Why don't you pay me after the race?"

"Thanks!" He smiles a mouthful of rotten teeth at us, and off they go. The guy went out in the race and made ten laps before the engine went down belching smoke and oil. But they were there, right after the last feature, fifteen dollars and 69 cents in hand.

"What can I do for you?" says Nils, shutting the back of his truck.

"I owe you for the plugs."

"What plugs?"

"I bought plugs from you..."

"Nope, I didn't sell any plugs tonight."

Ollie was parked next to us that night.

"Go on kid, he's doing you a favor... get lost."

"Yes sir, thanks..."

And the legend that I was a part of and didn't even recognize started to grow.

"Now, Reggie," (They all called him Reggie, Regnell being too foreign for their taste.) "about those plugs I bought from you... hey Mike, give Reggie twenty bucks, will you? I bought some plugs from him."

"Huh? We didn't buy any plugs..."

"Mike... I said I bought some plugs... pay the man."

"Sure Ollie, no problem."

In 1980, Ollie lost his touch and ran his super into the wall coming out of the second turn at Star Speedway. He wasn't killed; he even came back to race one more season — but it wasn't the same.

He is still suave and good looking, his hair is still black with a touch of gray at the temples. But his eyes are those of a stranger and his speech is halting. And every once in a while he loses track of what you are talking about and you have to remind him.

And quietly, in private moments in small groups, the guys remark that perhaps it would have been better if he had died.

They don't much like their heroes to be human.

Howard Brown died before his car hit the wall at Hudson. The heart attack he suffered claimed him before the wreckage burst into flames, but not before he watched his oldest son burn to death in a crash at Lee Speedway the year before. They say something went out of the 'Old Man' after that; they say he drove like he was trying to get himself killed.

And Junior Landry gave up racing. He said he was too busy in public, but in private he admitted that too many of the old crowd had died or worse behind the wheel.

We don't spend all our Saturdays between April and October at race tracks anymore. Nils is still into racing, but along with his business, his legend has also grown. He plays in the big boys' league now... sponsors 'Clean Car Awards' at the Northern NASCAR races and gets to wine and dine with guys like Petty and Allison when they come North.

And these days, when he stops by a small track, the guys in the pits go all quiet just like they used to for Ollie and Armand. And now, he is one of the folks who stops by someone's hauler or truck and sits to have a chat before he moves on.

And, I notice that it's race season again.

A guy was killed last weekend at Beech Ridge Speedway.

He brought his late-model onto the track and made two laps before his accelerator jammed and he roared into the wall on the third turn. The roll-cage that was there to protect him collapsed and crushed him. It took them three hours to pry his body from the wreckage, so *SportsWay Scene* said. They had a moment of silence on the start line in his memory; and then they went racing.

I didn't recognize his name. Somehow, that bothered me.

A Question of Ethics

Melinda Regnell

The first moments...

Borderline pregnant? What the hell is borderline pregnant?

That was what they told me I was just a few minutes ago. Considering the emotional trauma riding on the results of this particular question, borderline was not what I was looking for.

I mean how does one do 'borderline' pregnant? I always thought pregnant was one of those things that was relatively black and white... you know... you either were or you weren't. A case where almost doesn't count. Well, goes to show you once again how much I know about things.

I am being glib. I know it. You know it. Hiding from my fear and grief over an event that should never have happened, and did anyway. Somewhere, God is chuckling at my feeble attempts to control this little part of my destiny. I hope she is enjoying herself...

And I struggle with what I will do about it.

It is not as if we could not afford another child; it is not as if we could not love another child; it is not as if I am in mortal danger of dying from delivering another child; not as if it isn't my husband's... all the reasons for terror to stalk the recipient of such news are painfully missing from my personal dilemma.

I merely do not want another child. It would discommode me. What a naked statement. But if I am to make this decision, I had best face my real reasons. And, that is it. Not now, not ever again, for whatever reasons... no.

Kristin, God bless her, is here with tears in her eyes telling me that although she is not in very good shape herself these days, she will come with me so I do not have to be alone if I choose to abort. It is something, she says, that I should not have to ask... and she is right... I perhaps could not have. And, if I choose to do that, I will need her to help me cry.

I realize I am staring at the phone.

The first hours...

David, my lovable chameleon in California, a sometime lover and friend, an always unpredictable narcissist, is all of a sudden a bulwark of sympathy and strength. He is exhibiting even compassion, which is an emotion I truly thought he lacked for all that I care very deeply about him. He is a manic soul that desires love without having to give it back. Someday he will learn the only way to get it is to give it away, but I am too tired today to argue with him anyway. But there he is, holding my virtual hand across 3000 miles of telephone wires while I act inane and teary-eyed without so much as batting an eyelash. This is not the David I know... and yet, this is the David I love. I am reminded that my sixth sense is a better judge of men than I ever was...

And Steve. I should be pleased in some funny sort of way; I never hoped to catch him totally off guard. The look on his face when I told him of my latest fiasco was one of disbelief followed by hysterical denial and then love. All the right answers, dear, even in the right order. Without missing a beat he offered support, a shoulder to cry on, a place to hide... whatever I needed... including silence if that was what I needed. I am not surprised by his reaction... he has long been a person I counted upon for wisdom. I do still suspect that he overrates my handle on the universe, but right now, when I am feeling so completely out of control, his assurance that I am handling this well and wisely is a crutch I need very badly. I am content just to believe him this time. If he notices that my standard denial is missing, he has the grace to ignore it. He is a person that I share secrets with... a trusted confidant. I will need him in these days and weeks ahead.

And my mystery person, Bob. He who reads my essays and is fascinated by my view of the universe. He who had no idea of what was going on in the background. I called him to hear his voice and talk nonsense... to remind myself that this thing in me does not define who I am. I think he might be appalled by my probable course of action... then again I think not... then again, thinking is undoubtedly not my strong suit right this moment. He says I have a unique way of looking at things... I am hunting for inspiration right now and not finding any. We chat about Nova Scotia and old songs and my mother. I don't ever talk about Mother to anyone. As I carry on this spatially separated conversation, I realize that I never called her Mom, only Mother. I want desperately to hang on to that thought, it means something and I am going to write about it, but I have only the strength right now to remember the single thing. Oh my, wouldn't she just have a fit if she knew what plans are forming in my mind? I suspect she would hate me for it, if she does not already hate me for past refusals to play life by her rules. I hang up. I do not think he knew I was walking the edge of hysteria... unfortunately he will also never know I wanted to thank him for being him and for taking time to talk to me.

Nils. Somehow I thought this would be more difficult. Not in ways you might think... he is totally supportive. He does not want me to journey this road again... it was too terrifying the first times when we failed; too close to death the one time we succeeded. We have had enough of death this past year; he does not want to test the waters again. It is of me that his suggestions speak... never of himself and his possible desires. The questions that any man who has at least been trying to practice non-fertile sex for the past eight years has a right to think (if not say) are so obviously not even present in his mind that I want to hug him until he bursts. I am reminded that his faults are non-existent when compared with his virtues. He is simply a 'good' man. I am grateful he is mine.

Me? I think my mind kicked back in here somewhere. Perhaps when Eric crawled up in bed to hug me good night. I realize that I love him no less for not wanting to see if I can produce his likes again; that I am not denying motherhood by not wanting to populate my world with multiple children.

Sleep can be a sometime thing at times. I remember the other times I have sat out the darkness. When they took Eric to Boston in an ambulance when he was two weeks old and we couldn't follow until the next morning; when Claire's boyfriend died in Alabama and she and I sat in New Hampshire hearing the news on the phone; when the cat recently birthed four kittens and needed someone to pant with her; and a bright fall day when Nils was in Tennessee and his father was dying in New Hampshire. In the dark this night, it strikes me that I am most human, and therefore vulnerable at these times. Perhaps that is why I always sit in the dark. I remember my Dad telling me that if I was afraid or if there was someone in the house that was threatening me... I should turn off all the lights because it was my house... I knew it and the enemy would not. I would have the advantage. Is that what I do here in the dark... avoid the enemy? But what do I do when the enemy is me?

It also strikes me that I have spent these minutes and hours touching the people I care for. [No, that was not the word I wanted... I was going to say love, but that perhaps might offend one or two of them who do not buy into my rather broad, albeit sincere, use of the term.] I had to reach out to prove to myself that I am real and still whole... I feel disconnected like I am about to watch myself do something. All those people seem to think I am still Melinda; so perhaps I am.

The next day...

I spent today being busy. I did call the doctor's office and cancel my knee-jerk reaction appointment for this afternoon. I have to have a serum test next Tuesday to ascertain the real truth of the situation... so I really don't have anything to talk about until the results of the second test. I have all sorts of things to kick and scream and cry about, but my friends and lovers can get me through that; I will need my female doctor to get me through the details of my impending actions.

I spent today with Eric.

And I spent today with me. Thinking slower thoughts.

And, I spent today hefting furniture around a newly torn apart kitchen, washing floors, vacuuming, heaving trash hither, thither, and yon... to keep from thinking when my thoughts threatened to race ahead of me.

And Then, Tonight...

There of course was more to it than that. But my Daddy, he told me that if you told your dreams they might never come true; that they had to be secret; that you shouldn't even admit some of them to yourself. That's what my Daddy told me. And, although when I am safe and warm I understand at least parts of the personal desperation behind those words... and understand that what Daddy didn't know was that dreams are perhaps the one thing you should share with the people you love; when I am alone and terrified, I never tell my dreams.

I have a... what they call... a history.

Pregnancy comes easy to me; and seldom stays. Not a thing to bet on, but I have had more than would seem my share of miscarriages. No, not a thing to plan on so one does not make plans; but certainly a thing to remember.

I remembered quite clearly when I finally kept Eric, for the first three months I was under strict orders from our old family doctor to sit at all possible moments; lay down a good deal of the time; and lift nothing heavier than a fork. After three months things were pretty stable, but I shake loose very easily early on.

The pains started about the time I was moving the refrigerator. I guess it weighs about 300 pounds or so. But, my Daddy taught me how to get around problems like that; you just attack them from an oblique angle. I moved it. And after I got it where I wanted it, I went in the bathroom and washed the blood out of my clothes and took a shower.

It's a matter of ethics. I find that supporting a woman's right to control her destiny and her body is a theoretical necessity whereas actually allowing someone to take action to remove the whisper of life from my womb is a practical abhorrence. Do not misread me, I would have done it. It was the right thing to do. On the other hand, cleaning my kitchen is neither theoretical nor practical... it is a state of reality I can live with far easier.

I sat out the darkness of one more night... my mind is capable of splitting the hairs of rhetorical argument far more readily than my heart, but by tomorrow, I will be at ease. And if I should occasionally find inappropriate tears in my eyes over the next days we will count it against hormonal hysteria. And if there is a God, she will have to decide my penance another day.

Out of Darkness

Melinda Regnell

A thank you for Bob Johnson

A reader called me today. I have not written anything in a long time and I did not expect to hear from him. But he wasn't calling me about my essays, he was calling me about Don Murray's essays. The ones he writes in the Boston Globe in a column entitled 'Over Sixty'. I read them now and then, they are often exquisitely to the point and always beautifully crafted, and sometimes so close to the bone that reading them is like confession... or like what confession should be if the Catholic Church had not defiled it... but I wander. My reader called me to ask me a question.

He wanted to know, simply, if the man who wrote such evocative prose in the Boston paper was the man I had written about in my own essay, 'Teacher, Teacher', if the man to whom I attributed what little skill I own [my reader, of course, did not phrase the evaluation of my writing in that manner, but I seek to be humble on his account... a useless and self-seeking exercise at best] was this man writing in our local paper.

A simple "yes," of course, would have sufficed to answer the question. But the answer is very much more than what it seems.

Because, I noticed sunshine today. I haven't noticed it in some time. I am sure it has been there, I mean, I would have noticed six months of total darkness; but I just haven't had any interest in noticing that it was. Before today I spent time doing things that I never really thought people did. Contemplating one's navel, for example.

My doctor was not in the office; her husband was. Normally, I would have chosen to wait for a day when she was in, but somewhere inside something had snapped and I needed to know NOW what the pains meant... not tomorrow. Her husband is a good looking man, almost pretty. I distrusted him on sight.

"When did the pains start?"

"Oh, I don't know... they just sort of got bad enough to notice, you know?"

"Does it hurt here?"

"No."

"And here?"

"No."

"What about here?"

"No."

He sighed. I vaguely wondered if he was disappointed that it didn't hurt. I had been ticking off the answers mentally, tallying my score, thinking how perfectly I was doing because it didn't hurt, and here I was, finding out that the scoring system was backwards. It was supposed to hurt and it didn't. That scared me.

"I can't find anything wrong."

"This is bad? Or does that mean I'm making it up?"

"Perhaps neither. I think the pain is real, I just don't see any reason for it to be there. Your heart is fine, your pulse is fine, your breathing is normal... everything looks wonderful."

"And it hurts."

"Exactly. Have you ever tried tranquilizers?"

I slipped the side of my blouse up my arm and started buttoning it. "When did you say your wife would be back?"

He had the grace to look embarrassed.

"She keeps telling me to be sensitive with her female patients, and I keep thinking I am. I blew it, huh?"

"Very nearly."

"You have had a bad experience with tranquilizers, I take it?"

"Yes. I was told I was the 'nervous' type and the tranquilizer would make it better."

"And?"

"I still had all the symptoms I started with, I just didn't care any more that I couldn't swallow and felt like I was choking. Or that the car was 'that' close to sliding off an embankment... or that the kid who just ran into the street was a little too close to the car for comfort. I took one. The rest went down the toilet. I do not need to be dulled... I need to understand what is going on so I can actively work at correcting it."

"Unusual."

"Fine. Your wife...?"

"Mmm... oh, next week. In the meantime try hot and cold packs on your chest. I can reassure you about what it isn't, anyway."

He looked like Michael Fogg in first year Latin when he told Madam Downing that at least he hadn't missed all of the translations on the homework assigment.

I smiled rather frostily and left.

Navels. They come in all shapes... I suppose you know that? I used to call mine a belly button. I am not sure I have ever seen a navel that looked like a button. I have seen several that look like sailor's knots riding an invisible hole in the middle of a sea of abdomen; and I have seen some that look like an aborted appendage... like God decided at the very last instant that we didn't need a thumb in the middle of our stomachs... and I have seen some that looked like little lop-sided smiles without noses and eyes... but never have I seen one that looked like a button.

But I wore a button on mine every night for some interminably long time when I was six. Other people remember their first popsickle or their first movie or riding the pony at their cousin's. I remember laying on the kitchen table after the dinner dishes were done every night, Mother and Father hovering over me with the round kitchen light shining down in my eyes. Mother would take a ball of cotton and push it into the back of this concave yellow button. [I can't imagine what possible garment could have sported that button. I think there must be a market for buttons never meant to be attached to anything. They get bought solely for the purpose of filling button boxes.]

Then Daddy would rip two narrow pieces of adhesive tape off the red, white and blue metal roller. [Actually, he would rip one piece off and then rip that in two length-wise; why waste money buying multiple widths?] Then Mother would push in on my navel and Daddy would tape the button, cotton side down over it. Somewhere between then and now, I found out that I had a small hernia and the Doctor had told them to do this every night until it healed. At the time I was convinced that if I laid on my stomach or sneezed, my insides would pop out of my belly button.

A week of shooting pains and sometime-sleep passed. My doctor is of the black Irish persuasion... fair of skin and bone... black hair and eyes. Her skin always reminds me of parchment paper... I keep thinking if I look closely, I will be able to see through it to the blood vessels beneath. She is also direct and thankfully free of gratuitous niceties.

"Ok... what's bothering you?"

"Dizzy, disoriented, chest pains, vertigo, claustrophobia... my eyes wobble..."

"Wobble?"

"Shake so I can't focus."

"How long?"

"A second or two."

"And after?"

"Adrenalin... exhaustion."

"When did you stop speaking in full sentences?"

"When I started having to hold my skin on from the inside."

"How much stress are you under lately?"

"Oh, aside from my marriage falling apart and the company I work for doing massive layoffs and my projects demanding sixty hour weeks for weeks in a row... not much."

"Sleep?"

"Never enough... but hard to get there."

"Weight, sex?"

"Gaining and losing."

"Well, you are in a fine mess, aren't you?"

I looked at her and knew that there was humor in her eyes and concern behind it. And the most frightening thing I could think of was that I didn't particularly care.

"What do you think you need?"

"Time."

"That I can do. In the meantime, I want to run some tests. You are off work now, today... for at least three weeks."

I never thought I would remember that yellow button. But it swims back to the surface at odd times, reminding me of my imperfection.

I remembered it the day after I had Eric by Caesarean section and the disgustingly cheerful nurse who looked old enough to be at least 17 and didn't have a stretch mark anywhere on her body burbled at me to, "get up and move around."

Neophyte that I was, I moved to get up. My belly felt exactly like it did all those nights when they taped the button on it... just like it was going to fall out on the floor. The only difference was that this time it hurt like hell at the same time. And there was that little nurse flitting around like some cheerful little bumblebee. If I had had the wherewithal I would have smacked her up the side of the head. But I didn't. I just waited for my guts to spill out on the floor. Miraculously they didn't. But they continued to feel like they would for weeks... even after the stitches were out I would roll to my feet gingerly to prevent the abrupt strain from bursting me open like a ripe pop-weed pod.

My little Campfire Girl brain searched its memory banks for precautions to take if one's insides spilled out. I recalled my seventh grade science teacher asking a spell-bound class what we should do if we chanced upon an accident victim whose belly had been ripped open. [I assumed this action was to follow immediately after vomiting into the grass.] As several adolescent girls paled to the brink of swooning, she explained that we should get a wet sheet [from where I have no idea... perhaps we were supposed to carry a clean sheet and a gallon of water with us everywhere we went] and drape it over the entrails to keep them malleable. [Make that two gallons of water.] My personal assessment of the class was that there were only one or two who would still be conscious after seeing the victim, so I wondered why she was telling us this.

Under cover of rearranging the bedding trunk, I found and moved to a more prominent position the single white sheet I owned. I must have been subconsciously preparing for this emergency for years, as I didn't own another white piece of bedding or even have a bed small enough for the sheet to go over. Silently congratulating myself on my foresight, I tucked it away in back of the towels in the bathroom, so I could get to it quickly.

When the insanity of early motherhood passed, along with the disconcerting feeling of everything inside me shifting when I leaned over, I quietly removed my safety sheet and put it back in the bottom of the bedding trunk. I didn't throw it out. Just because my insides were no longer in danger of erupting onto my kitchen floor didn't mean someone else's might not. [I think it's genetic... the gift of imagining all possible catastrophes coupled with the inability to disregard the most improbable.]

Don Murray was so much more than just the man who taught me to write. But somehow, even in my mind, I am unable to categorize exactly what he was to me. Teacher, mentor, whip-cracker... all when I needed it.

And here was a reader of mine telling me that Don's latest essay reminded him of my essays. If I had planned for this day, I would have expected to swoon at the very words... do cartwheels down the aisles... foam at the mouth or some other equally exuberant activity. But instead, I feel great sorrow.

"Well, you're healthy as an ox."

"Is an ox healthy?"

"Your cholesterol is 142, your blood sugar is normal, you don't have AIDS, you have no other communicable diseases..."

"So why can't I function?"

"Do you know anything about depression?"

"No." I had this sinking feeling that yet another doctor was going to tell me I was a nut case. And this one was female. My hopes of finally having found a woman doctor who didn't try to pawn every pain and ache off as PMS or whim-and-frenzy was fading.

"It has nothing to do with being depressed. It is a stupid name for the real condition."

"What condition?"

"It is a lack of a chemical in the brain."

I looked as confused as I was.

"This chemical, seratonin, carries messages between nerve endings that are responsible for keeping your body functioning. When there isn't enough to go around, things start to slip... you aren't as quick mentally, your muscles may ache... you get quick tempered"

That sounded like me, all right. "So, what can I do about it?"

"The brain will eventually produce enough of the chemical and 'catch up' if you let it rest long enough."

"Well..."

"I am assuming that we can't keep you out of work for the next four months while it rests, so we will try some medicines that stimulate seratonin production. The one I want to use, I won't. It has had too much bad press. But I want to try one first that is much like it."

So. I spent several weeks re-thinking my attitude on navels. It fascinated me. Well, as far as I could be fascinated, anyway.

I graduated somewhere around about three weeks into being interested in my son's Nintendo games. Obsessed with them in fact. I spent thirteen hours one day trying to get past the second level of Super Mario Brothers Two. Somewhere around the eleventh hour, it penetrated my addled brain that I was lacking some elemental ingredient for success at this task. I gave up before I figured out whether it was co-ordination or the will to win that I lacked, thank God.

And I spent some time staring at the wall. I don't think I have ever seen a truly straight wall. They buckle or sway, or ripple around corners in ambush for the uninititated wallpaper hanger or a challenge for the experienced one. Why do you suppose we have walls? We walk around them, listen through them, knock holes through them [if you are like me] to put doors into. I came up with the only definitive answer while I was staring at them... to hold up ceilings, of course... for those of us addicted to multi-storeyed buildings.

And finally, around the fifth week or so, I actually began to notice the world around me again. It is a painfully slow process. There are days when I still don't care and don't want to move and the thought of doing three things at once can literally send me into a panic attack. I was very proud of myself this week, I actually went to dinner with some friends. Of course, they were friends I trusted, the kind that will pick you up if you should faint... or hold you up if you should start to buckle... and act like it was all part of the planned agenda for the evening while doing so. But I went, and that was the important part. My first 'date' in nine months.

After my reader called, I went and dug out the *Boston Globe* to read the piece he had noted. It was titled 'The Art That Saves Us From Ourselves' and seemed to be about writing but wasn't. Just like the phone call seemed to be about telling me that my writing reminded my reader of Don Murray's writing but wasn't. It was obvious that Don is ill. Oh, the writing was as fine as ever, but the meanderings stopped by places that the actively healthy do not visit, and there was a 'taking-stock' feel to it that I have not noticed in his material before. I read it three times.

Then I rushed out and bought a mailing envelope and stuffed a painstakingly gathered collection of my essays [a birthday present from a dear friend] into it along with an apology for waiting so long to say thank you for the magic he gave me in person.

And then I sat down to write this little piece. Another thank you, of a sort, for the reader who under the guise of delivering a compliment let me know that it was time to return to the world... time to notice a dear friend and mentor who was ill... time enough to say thank you before time itself turned good intentions into words whispered to ghosts in graveyards.

Thank you, dear reader.

Tripping Up Snakes

Neil Ambrose

The sun rose over a dreary North London landscape that frankly looked better in the dark. As the grubby Victorian mansions and their puddled backyards were slowly revealed, the sun — as if having second thoughts — slid into a comfy cloud where it could remain all day. These early morning solar shenanigans were observed as usual by Mary Reagan who sat in her kitchen smoking king size cigarettes and drinking milky coffee.

Winter or summer, spring or autumn, Mary awoke every morning at 5am. Sleep did not come easily to Mary, and once she lost her grip sleep was as elusive as a greased goldfish. At first she had tried to fight against the sleeplessness and had sought advice from doctors, friends, strangers she cornered at parties, and customers at the bar where she worked the day shift. And the advice had been as plentiful as the sleep had been lacking — but warm milk made her pee, pills made her rattle and vodka made her giggle. Once in desperation she took a cocktail of all three which led to her having her stomach pumped and a paragraph in the local paper. The paper misspelt her name and added three years to her age. When she phoned to complain a snide young man told her that having her stomach pumped was nothing to be proud of and if it hadn't been such a quiet week they wouldn't have run the story anyway. He then put down the phone. Hard.

So now Mary let nature take its course and used the hours before the rest of the world awoke to think her thoughts and pick at the table-top Formica. Mary was, in her own opinion, a mighty fine thinker. Not a Nobel prize winner perhaps, or even Olympic standard, but a good amateur. She had stamina, she was determined. The hole in the Formica had grown over the years as Mary picked at it with her nails trying to persuade it into a regular shape. But each time it was close to being a near-as-damnit perfect circle, a larger piece than expected would snap off and the hole would resemble something as ridiculous as Bob Hope's profile.

Had Mary's thoughts been of a more literary bent she may have drawn a parallel between the hole in the Formica and her life per se. But instead her thoughts were of a more practical nature, such as painting the front door, growing her own vegetables and leaving her husband. But like all the great thinkers her thoughts remained as thoughts and nothing more. The front door remained blistered and peeling, the vegetables came pre-packed in plastic and she would still be with her husband now if he hadn't stolen the initiative away from her and not returned from the betting shop one afternoon. For three months Mary had no idea of what might have become of him. She imagined him being snatched by blue-skinned extra-terrestrials with ten fingers on each hand as a sex-slave (boy, would they be disappointed) or falling into the mechanical jaws of a council dust-cart. Then out of the blue she received a badly spelt letter in his familiar untidy scrawl asking her to forward his second-best suit and any spare money that she didn't want to an address in Wolverhampton. "Poor, poor man," thought Mary as she flushed the roughly torn pieces of letter down the lavatory pan.

The purr of the milk float in the street below announced the start of the day. The clink-clink of milk bottles would soon wake the light sleepers and the shrill shriek of bedside alarms would penetrate the fathoms to call to those sunk deeper in slumber. Mary hung her thoughts on a hook on the back of the kitchen door and prepared herself for the day ahead.

Mary loved her job in the Old Shillelagh and she loved the customers. She loved the way their hands dangled below their knees and the way they approached the bar by executing a series of heavy little hops. Evolution stood sulking in the shadows by the wall, like a plain girl at a country dance; an option waiting to be taken up.

The atmosphere in the bar had a comforting, if potentially lethal, high smoke to oxygen ratio. The carpet was ash grey, the walls nicotine yellow, and the ceiling could never be seen. A sign pinned to the pub door said 'No Unusual Pets' but truth be told a herd of elk could mingle unnoticed amongst the regular clientèle so thick was the fog. As she stood behind the bar, Mary had almost succeeded in convincing herself that she must resemble a pre-Raphaelite maiden, lost in the mists of an enchanted forest, at the mercy of trolls and evil dwarfs, waiting to be rescued by a gallant knight, heroic in stature and heroic in nature, a demi-god upon a tall white steed.

"That's me, that is," announced a voice, causing Mary to start.

"What?" she asked.

"This is me," insisted a short fat man in a donkey jacket, jerking his short fat head towards the ceiling.

"What is?"

"On the jukebox. It's me. Singing."

"Eddie Cochran?"

"That's me. Eddie Cochran."

"Eddie Cochran is dead."

"No I'm not. I'm fit as a fiddle." He leant forward conspiratorially and placed his elbow in a pool of stale lager. "I saw Elvis the other day," he said.

"And what did he have to say for himself?"

"Not a lot. He was washing the car. Can I tell you about my near-death experience?"

Fortunately for the sake of Mary's sanity, at that moment the door of the bar crashed open and her good friend Tom Doherty strode in. "Mary, Mary, Mary, Mary, Mary!" he called.

Tom wore a voluminous trench coat that would have fitted him better if he stood on another man's shoulders. As he made his way towards the bar the coat billowed out behind him and swept half a pint of Guinness, a large Irish whiskey, an ashtray, a chess set and a packet of potato crisps off a small table and into the lap of a sleeping geriatric.

"Hello, Tom," said Mary. "I hear that you and Theresa are back together again."

"I was on the operating table," continued Eddie Cochran, "and I had a near-death experience."

"We are yes. I bought her a dog. A greyhound. A lovely creature. It's given her back the will to live. She cried when she saw it. Ask her. She'll tell you I've given her back the will to live."

"I floated above my body and I heard this voice saying 'Are you ready to die yet?'"

"I'm very pleased for you, Tom."

"And I said 'No I'm not,' and the voice said 'Why not?' and I said 'I've got a sick mother,' and the voice said 'So what?'".

"She calls the dog Mahatma Ghandi. Heaven knows why. When you're finished here Mary we'll go and visit Theresa and the dog. I'll meet you at seven."

"And the voice said, 'We want you to go from door to door spreading the word of God, and warning against the evils of sin, etc., etc.' So I said, 'Ooh, that sounds interesting'. Well you would wouldn't you."

"I'm not sure, Tom."

"Are you two listening to me?"

"What?"

"What?"

"I've seen Pat Boone naked."

Theresa's house. The end of a small Islington terrace. On the steps of the church opposite two teenage girls sat whispering secrets and sharing a cigarette.

"Sorry, girls, I'm already spoken for!" called Tom, leaning casually on the front doorbell. The girls blushed and giggled, the door opened, and Tom stumbled into the hallway. His shoes tangled in the folds of his raincoat and he fell flat on his face on the man-made fibre. A growling, slavering greyhound shot from the back room and sank his teeth into the tails of Tom's coat.

"What the hell are you doing here?" demanded Theresa.

"Just checking the carpet, my sweet," said Tom, pathetically, as he scrambled to his feet, the dog swinging from his coat-tails.

"Playful little fellow, isn't he?" Tom aimed a kick at Mahatma Ghandi's midriff but Mahatma ducked and weaved and Tom's size nine missed by miles. "Do you have a kiss for the man in your life?"

"The good lord Jesus is the only man in my life, you sinner. Now get your arse out of here."

"Amen, Theresa. But what the hell are you talking about? Have you been at the bottle again?"

Tom turned to Mary for some support, but Mary was already fifty yards down the street and moving fast. Mahatma Ghandi barked like a maniac around Tom's ankles and curtains twitched as the neighbours peered through their windows to get a better look.

"No more than enough to rinse the taste of you from my lips," said Theresa. "I was visited today by a messenger from the Lord. A charming man; he had a near death experience. He has shown me the light. I repent and I seek salvation. You, Tom, will burn in Hell."

"I don't like your incinerations, Theresa. Now give me three good reasons why you don't want me around. I can be very useful about the house. Let me stay the night and we can talk things over."

"You've the morals of an alley cat and the intellect of a sponge. Now drop dead, Tom, and do us both a favour."

The dog let out a strangled yelp as Theresa dragged it in by the collar and slammed the door.

"Couldn't think of three reasons though, could you?" shouted Tom through the letter box.

"And you're a clumsy git!" came the muffled reply.

Tom was smiling as only a man who has been abused and insulted and savaged by a greyhound can smile when he eventually caught up with Mary. "It's her loss, Mary. It's her loss. Jesus never spent a hundred quid on a greyhound like I did. Ungrateful, that's what she is. Not like you Mary. You're the sort of woman that I need."

"And what sort might that be?"

"Friendly, Mary. Friendly, basically. Friendly and homely. The sort that would rather raise rabbits than hell. Friendly and homely with pale skin and lovely apple cheeks. A milky nymph with apple cheeks. That's the sort you are."

"You have a silver tongue, Tom, though you make me sound like a pudding. Carry on like this and I might start taking you seriously. I might even believe you. So take care."

"But I do mean it Mary. Why don't we get married? I'll buy you a dog."

Mary laughed and her laughter turned to steam in the early autumn evening air.

"Would that be wise, Tom?" she said. "Now, would that be wise?"

Midnight. Mary sat at her kitchen table smoking cigarettes and drinking coffee. Before her lay the remains of her supper and a torn cardboard container. Mary checked the box for a clue as to what she had just eaten. 'Slimline Antelope with Baby Elephants,' she read. "Perhaps I should go for an eye-test," she thought. "Perhaps I'll get some glasses."

Outside the air was full of night-time London sounds — the low hum of traffic, police car sirens, and the plaintive cries of horny cats. Somewhere in the distance a drunk sang the first verse of 'A Hard Day's Night' over and over and over. As she crushed out her cigarette, Mary caught sight of her reflection in the window. A milky nymph in a Marks & Spencer night-dress. She stuck out her tongue and pulled a face. The nymph grimaced back. "Friendly and homely is no bad thing to be," thought Mary, "especially when combined with apple cheeks. Better, say, than being naked in a tower-block with a photo of the Pope and a high-powered rifle."

Abandoning the dishes until the morning, Mary wandered into the bathroom to clean and count her teeth. And then into the bedroom and into bed. Before turning of the light she checked that the alarm was set for 8.30. Just in case she overslept. Just in case.